A Gradual Awakening

A Gradual Awakening

STEPHEN LEVINE

ANCHOR BOOKS
A DIVISION OF RANDOM HOUSE, INC.
NEW YORK

ANCHOR BOOKS EDITIONS, 1979, 1989

Copyright © 1979, 1989 by Stephen Levine

All rights reserved under International and Pan-American Copyright
Conventions. Published in the United States by Anchor Books,
a division of Random House, Inc., New York, and simultaneously
in Canada by Random House of Canada Limited, Toronto.
Originally published in paperback in the United States
by Anchor Books in 1979.

Anchor Books and colophon are registered trademarks
of Random House, Inc.

ISBN 0-385-26218-3

Library of Congress Catalog Card Number 77-27712

www.anchorbooks.com

PRINTED IN THE UNITED STATES OF AMERICA
30 29 28 27 26 25 24 23 22 21

Acknowledgments

I would like to thank the following very much for their inspiration and participation:

Ram Dass, who first encouraged the creation of this book and has been so supportive of these teachings;

Jack Kornfield, whose fine heart and eye greatly aided the maturation of this transmission;

Al Strickland, whose enormous effort transcribing tapes and typing and retyping this manuscript allowed this book to become a reality;

Karen Dega, whose keen and loving criticism helped prune the manuscript;

Nancy Klebanova, whose generosity and friendship aided in the final stages of completion;

And, most of all, the Santa Cruz sangha, whose purity drew forth these teachings.

Contents

Preface for A Gradual Awakening

When my Guru wanted to compliment me, he called me simple; when he wished to chide me, he called me clever. This book about vipassana meditation is simple . . . clear and familiarly comfortable. It just is what is. This simplicity surprises me when I realize that the book deals with profound topics that I have often fruitlessly pondered in ancient tomes of Buddhist lore. I always knew in my heart that these matters were quite simple, and so it is a delight to see them so presented.

Besides its simplicity, there is another treasure in this book. It concerns social responsibility. There has always been a dialogue between the Mahayana and the Theravada Buddhists concerning social responsibility. Does one hold back from liberation in order to assist all sentient beings to end their suffering, or does one go for broke?

Although this debate involves numerous fine philosophical points, for most of us it seems rather academic. Our problem is not one of holding back liberation: rather, day by day we patiently struggle to extricate ourselves from the vast, clinging karmic web in which we are enmeshed.

So for us the issue of social responsibility is a daily matter of whether to sit or serve, to retreat or leap into the fray.

Again and again I am asked how I can justify sitting in meditation while there is so much suffering going on all about me. The intellectual answer is that the root of suffering is ignorance and that meditation is the best way of cutting the bonds of ignorance. But when confronted with a hungry child, the pains of physical illness, the intractable violence in others, or the fear of dying, such justifications sometimes seem dissatisfyingly abstract and hollow.

Stephen Levine deals with meditation and social responsibility in a way that is neither abstract nor hollow: This is practical stuff for day-to-day living. His ability to do this comes from his own life in which he has shown a continuing sense of social consciousness.

I first met Stephen in the early days of Haight-Ashbury when he edited the *San Francisco Oracle*, which was among the first voices of the consciousness awakening of the sixties. Later I knew him as a poet, as an articulate friend of and spokesman for the men on death row at San Quentin, as a successful editor-publisher, as a father of two superb children, and most recently as a companion-guide to those who would approach death as an opportunity to awaken. And through all of this he has continued to deepen his meditative practice and to carry the resulting clarity of mind into his social action.

And there is one more jewel of which I would recommend that the reader take note. It is the weaving of the domains of heart and mind. So often spiritual practices have emphasized the false dichotomy between practices of the heart and practices of the mind. Much of this confusion is due to defining the heart space in terms of emotions, and to considering pure mind as rather antiseptically dry. Of course such polarization is naïve, but it too often catches us. Thus it is refreshing to see in both the Metta meditation and the discussion which follows, a sensitive mind-heart integration that allows for both a moist warmth and a clear spaciousness.

Buddhism is often referred to as the Middle Way. Some meditation books are for the beginner who has never really thought of meditating; some books are for the advanced practitioner. *A Gradual Awakening* would seem most beneficial to those in the middle stages of the Middle Way. That is, readers who realize there is a journey and have embarked upon it. To them, I wish Godspeed.

May all beings realize liberation.

RAM DASS

Introduction

Twenty years ago I sat in great confusion before a plaster dime-store Buddha and asked to be taught how to meditate. I discovered a few early translations of Buddhist texts and the first encouraging works of D. T. Suzuki and Alan Watts, but there was no actual method offered for the direct experience of these truths. Often I had the frustrating feeling of reading a travelogue of some extraordinary terrain I wished to visit but for which no access map was available.

It was a few years before I met Rudi, my first teacher, sitting at his desk in the back of an oriental art shop in New York City. Twice a week for the next several months he pointed out various states of mind as illustrated in the faces of passers-by as we sat on folding chairs before his shop on Seventh Avenue. Repeatedly he told me to let go of my thinking mind, but instead I analyzed and sifted his words, I sought "meaning" instead of freedom. I could not hear the Buddha in either of us.

My pull to Theravada (the Way of the Elders) and Zen Buddhism continued without the benefit of a teacher or any but an intuitive method of self-exploration. Slowly I was acquiring a way of thinking, but nothing more profound or useful.

Then, in the mid-sixties, a friend returning from study in Burma brought with him a booklet of instructions in *vipassana*, the mindfulness or insight method of Buddhist meditation. He said that of all the teachings he had received in four years as a Buddhist monk, this simple meditation was the most useful. These teachings by the much respected Burmese meditation master Mahasi Sayadaw immediately drew me into deeper practice and discovery.

Working with the method described in this booklet, I established a rather irregular practice over the next few years, until I met a young Theravadin Buddhist monk who offered me more complete instruction and guidance. By helping me to acknowledge the conditioning and confront the blind spots which had made practice without a teacher a slower and often less enthusiastic commitment, he led me to the establishment of an ongoing practice.

After a couple of years of work with this young monk, I met Jack Kornfield and Joseph Goldstein, two accomplished insight meditation teachers with whom I have continued to practice and who first encouraged me to begin teaching three years ago.

I began to teach in Soledad Prison in 1976, and occasionally was able to tape record the groups. A few of these transcriptions were the basis for chapters included here. During this period, Ram Dass invited me to teach mindfulness meditation at his retreats, and soon we put together a book *Grist for the Mill.* At that point, the Hanuman Tape Library, distributor of Ram Dass's tapes, moved to Santa Cruz, and it seemed appropriate to begin weekly classes there. The greater part of this book is taken from transcriptions of these meetings. During this grace-filled time, Elisabeth Kübler-Ross invited me to teach with her at her workshops; there are various transcriptions included here from these gatherings as well.

These words are offered not as Absolute Truth, but rather as the outcome of a process of learning out loud. I offer this book to that confused fellow, sitting twenty years ago in his cottage in Florida, just dropped out of college, wondering which way to freedom.

Stephen Levine
Santa Cruz, California
August 1978

Author's Note
(1989)

When I wrote these somewhat dated words ten years ago, I had no idea that the work my wife, Ondrea, and I were doing was shared by so many. I had always published with small, enthusiastic West Coast publishers in limited editions and was surprised that a company as large as Doubleday was interested in publishing and widely distributing a book of meditation instruction.

As it turns out, it was the vision of Loretta A. Barrett, my editor for four books over the past ten years, who believed in our work and moved the first book through committee and into print. Since that time *A Gradual Awakening*—quite unexpectedly—has gone into more than a dozen printings and become a basic teaching text (along with *Who Dies?*) in meditation centers, hospitals, hospices, wellness groups, healing centers, and cancer and AIDS support groups across the country. The book continues to be used widely in schools, ranging from small-town junior highs to Harvard Medical School. For Ondrea and me, this consistent response to our work has been a further teaching in trust and a reminder that, as one of our great teachers, the Indian Saint Neem Karoli Baba, said, "When you do God's work, the work does it itself."

1

Awareness

Meditation is for many a foreign concept, somehow distant and foreboding, seemingly impossible to participate in. But another word for meditation is simply awareness. Meditation *is* awareness.

The motivation for meditating is often quite different for each person. Many people come to meditation because of their love for the qualities of some teacher or their desire to know God. Others because of a desire to understand mind. Some begin not even knowing what meditation is, but with a great longing to be free from some sadness, some pain, some incompleteness in their lives.

Here is offered a simple Buddhist mindfulness practice to come to wholeness, to our natural completeness. The basis of the practice is to directly participate in each moment as it occurs with as much awareness and understanding as possible.

We've all developed some degree of concentration and awareness. Just to be able to read a book, to live our complicated lives, takes awareness and concentration. They're qualities of mind present in everyone.

Meditation intensifies those qualities through systematic, gentle, persevering techniques. To develop concentration, we choose a single object of awareness, the primary object, that the attention is "re-minded" to return to and encouraged to stay with. A basic difference between various meditation forms—such as TM, or Sufi dancing, or confronting Zen koans, or sitting meditations, or Christian prayer, or chanting mantra, or listening to the inner sound current, or cycling light, or observing sensations in the body, or visualizing techniques, or watching the breath—is the primary object on which concentration is developed. We choose a primary object and work with it; whether it is something we generate in the conceptual realm, like a verbal repetition or the idea of loving-kindness, or something that is always present, like the sensations in the body.

Mindfulness of breathing is a powerful means of developing concentration. The breath is a superb object because it's constantly a part of our experience. Also, because our breathing changes, the awareness must become very subtle to accommodate itself to it. Awareness watches the sensations that occur with the natural coming and going of the breath. Awareness penetrates the subtle sensations that accompany each breath. When we bring attention to the level of sensation, we are not so entangled in the verbal level where all the voices of thought hold sway, usually lost in the "internal dialogue."

The internal dialogue is always commenting and judging and planning. It contains a lot of thoughts of self, a lot of self-consciousness. It blocks the light of our natural wisdom; it limits our seeing who we are; it makes a lot of noise and attracts our attention to a fraction of the reality in which we exist. But when the awareness is one-pointedly focused on the coming and going of the breath, all the other aspects of the mind/body process come automatically, clearly into focus as they arise. Meditation puts us into direct contact—which means direct experience—with more of who we are.

For instance, if we watch the mind as though it were a film projected on a screen, as concentration deepens, it may go into a kind of slow motion and allow us to see more of what is happening. This then deepens our awareness and further allows us to observe the film almost frame by frame, to discover how one thought leads imperceptively to the next. We see how thoughts we took to be "me" or "mine" are just an ongoing process. This perspective helps break our deep identification with the seeming solid reality of the movie of the mind. As we become less engrossed in the melodrama, we see it's just flow, and can watch it all as it passes. We are not even drawn into the action by the passing of a judgmental comment or an agitated moment of impatience.

When we simply see—moment to moment—what's occurring, observing without judgment or preference, we don't get lost thinking, "I prefer this moment to that moment, I prefer this pleasant thought to that pain in my knee." As we begin developing this choiceless awareness, what starts coming within the field of awareness is quite remarkable: we start seeing the root from which thought arises. We see intention, out of which action comes. We observe the natural process of mind and discover how much of what we so treasured to be ourselves is essentially impersonal phenomena passing by.

We discover we don't really need to ask anyone any questions, we needn't look outside ourselves for the answer.

As we penetrate the flow, the flow is the answer. The asking of the question is itself the answer. When we ask, "Who am I?" who we are is the processes asking the question.

When awareness penetrates a bit deeper, we discover that we've invested the thinking mind with a reality which it doesn't independently possess, an absolute reality, not understanding that it is a relative part of something much greater. By not being addicted to thinking, we discover that we usually notice only a bit of the extraordinary activity of consciousness; attachment to thinking has blocked the rest. Thinking mind is quite other than the choiceless, open awareness that allows everything to unfold as it must. Thinking is choosing thoughts, it's working, it's measuring, it's planning, it's creating a reality instead of directly experiencing what's actually happening each moment.

When we attend to the ongoing mind we see that even "the watcher" becomes part of the flow. The who that's asking "Who's watching?" is another thought-flash we see go by; there's "no one" watching, there's just awareness. When the "I" becomes just something else observed in the flow we see we're not different from anything else in the universe. The true nature of being becomes apparent because there's nothing to remain separate, nothing to block our totality. We see that what moves one thought into another is the exact same energy that moves the stars across the sky. No difference. We are natural phenomenon as full of change as the ocean or the wind, a product of conditions.

We see that the nature of consciousness works a bit like the hand of God in the famous Sistine Chapel painting which is reaching out to give life to a waiting being, a being about to receive the spark. Moment to moment we're receiving the spark. That spark is consciousness, the knowing faculty, the perception of which arises from the contact of awareness and its object; from sight and the tree seen, from hearing and the music heard, from touch and the earth felt, from taste and the water tasted, from smell and the flower smelled, from thought and the idea imagined. Moment to moment, consciousness arises anew in conjunction with each object of the senses, including the mind sense of imagination and memory. This is the arising and passing away of all that we know of our life experience. For mindfulness to enter this process is to discover genesis moment to moment, the continual creation of the universe.

Interestingly enough, it is this act of creation which is the greatest cause of misunderstanding in our life. Or to be more precise, it is our identification with this ongoing process as "I" which becomes the problem. It is the wrong view of this natural unfolding which forms the basis for most of our drowsy blindness and illusion. Consciousness results automatically from the contact of awareness and its object. This "knowing" is the result of a natural process which exists of itself without necessity of a "knower," or any added "I" which somehow supposes responsibility for this essentially non-personal process. This interposed "I" keeps us from participating in the direct experience of this flow, the direct experience of the universal nature of our being.

Aurobindo said, "To be fully is to be all that is." Experiences come and go. If we identify with them, claim them as "me" or "mine" by judging or clinging, if we stick to any part of the ongoing flow, we don't see that what we call "me" is constantly being born and dying, is a process of awareness and object coming into being and passing away hundreds of times each minute.

As awareness more deeply penetrates the flow, we experience that our natural condition, our natural state of being which some call the wisdom-mind or Buddha nature, is like the sun which is always shining, always present, though often obscured. We are blocked from our natural light by the clouds of thought and longing and fear; the overcast of the conditioned mind; the hurricane of "I am."

2

The Power of Wisdom

Often when we hear people speak about meditation, we hear about wisdom, we hear about knowledge. But what, actually, is the effect, what's the use, of wisdom or knowledge?

Understanding. When you understand mind, you're not at its mercy. When you don't understand, you're lost in the midst of it. It's the difference between being in bondage to thought or being liberated by it. There is a difference between wisdom and knowledge. We experience a moment of understanding and say, "Ah, that's how it is!" Then think "Now, how did that happen?" and perhaps later try to explain to others how it was. The experience of understanding is wisdom, but trying to capture that understanding, to convey it in words, is knowledge.

We all have knowledge. We can all convey a lot of very far-out ideas. But if wisdom does not precede the "knowing," then knowledge is secondhand, another's understanding, and lacks depth. That is why two people can use the same language to convey an idea, but one's words will penetrate deeply into our hearts while another's will just ricochet around in the mind. The power of the experience behind the words, the being behind the knowledge, is the wisdom, the real transmission.

For instance, a book may say that all beings are one. We think, "Sure, I can see how that's true: everybody's got a body, and everybody's got a mind, and everybody's got emotions, everybody eats food and breathes air; we all live on this planet. I understand what that means." Then during a moment of deep awareness we experience ourself as not being separate from anything else; in fact, there isn't even an "anything else" to be separate from. And we think, "Wow, we *really* are all one!" But, when we try to communicate the experience, we find ourselves saying, almost in exasperation, "We're all one." We are using the same words we had read before, but they're inadequate because the meaning has changed so drastically. It can't be communicated, it can only be experienced.

The purpose of this book is not to share knowledge, but to indicate that wisdom is available within each of us, and that the work of balancing the mind so that it can shine through is the work we must each do for and on ourselves. For me, this writing is part of my practice, and I have to make sure that I'm being honest myself. It's easy when our mouths are open to fall asleep. That's the time we most often are out cold: we are projecting who we think we are—we're projecting our games and opinions which keep deeper understanding from arising.

One aspect of the power of wisdom is its ability to cut through what we have previously thought to be real. Each time we learn something new, we discard an old opinion, we change opinions. But wisdom is a stillness, a light within, in which we see what opinions themselves are; not just this opinion as opposed to that opinion, but what "opinion-ism" is. Opinionism is just mind clinging to an idea. When we open to the wisdom mind we see how things are and say, "Well, look how things change."

Indeed, if we were to try to find a single truth all could agree on, it would perhaps be that everything changes. Opinions are constantly changing, mind is constantly changing, the body is constantly changing, the world is constantly changing, our relationships are constantly changing. As simple as that statement is, it has great wisdom. And wisdom is generally quite simple because it applies everywhere. The truth is the truth here, and it's the truth there. It's the truth in chemistry or physics or thermodynamics or psychology. Each is just a different form in which the same truth resides. It is like the truth of the law of karma, cause and effect, being equally manifest in Newton's laws of motion which state that for every force there is an equal and opposite force in the opposite direction. Because this truth may be expressed differently at different levels of experience it might seem paradoxical, but that is the difficulty of trying to hold wisdom in knowledge and the limitations of language.

When we start meditating it becomes very clear that everything is changing moment to moment. When we sit for even five minutes trying to keep the attention on the breath, we often think, "I can't keep my attention where I want it. It goes to this thought and then to that thought, and then to this sensation and then to that smell, then to some sound, and then. . . ." We notice that one thing after another comes before the mind's eye. We see it's all a flow of constant change, coming and going: each moment leading to the next.

This insight seems so simple that we may say that it's not even wisdom. But, when we deeply experience change, when we deeply understand that nothing is permanent, our wisdom grows. The next thing we discover is that nothing we want can give us lasting satisfaction because everything is in flux and nothing stays for ever. Whatever it may be—the finest food, the most gratifying sex, the greatest sense pleasure—nothing in the universe can give lasting satisfaction, it will all come and go. It is this condition which gives us that subtle, queasy dissatisfaction we carry about with us most of the time, even when we get what we want, because deep down we know eventually it will change.

It's not that we're the same and only the world is changing. We're part of the world. Mind is always changing. That's why we're happy one day and unhappy the next. It's not just outside things changing. Everything is changing, and that pulls against our concepts of how things are because our concepts are solid, imaginary things which don't reflect change. The concept of tree, for example, is one solid, steady thing; not a growing, changing organism, subtly different from any other of its species, altered by weather and exposure and conditions. We have stiff, unchanging conceptual labels in a world full of change which, of course, causes a split between the concept and the reality, and a resulting tension. We don't really see reality. We see only the shadows that it casts and those shadows are our concepts, our definitions, our ideas of the world. Clinging to these concepts creates a desire that the world reflect our idea of how it should be; but change often confronts our concepts with a much different reality than we imagined, and can cause us to feel angry or defeated; somehow isolated from the truth of things by our tightly held point of view.

In the midst of all this change it is interesting to note

that what we generally experience is not what is going on, but what we *think* about what's going on. Sitting and listening, we are not experiencing hearing. We are experiencing, to some degree, a running commentary on what is being said, perhaps a judgment or comparison with similar concepts, or a run of associated thoughts recalled by the conversation. At one level, of course, all that is actually happening is that sound is traveling through the air and striking our eardrums, and, because of memory and perceptual mechanisms, the mind is recognizing what is being said.

So we see that our experience is not of what's actually happening, but rather of the world of thought. Most of our experience is a dream-reflection in mind. We don't experience our seeing so much as what we think about what we're seeing, or our hearing so much as what we think about what we're hearing.

When this subject would come up during the classes I taught in Soledad Prison last year I would mention that if the men had smelled a waft of perfume right then, they wouldn't be experiencing that scent for an instant before the direct experience of smelling was buried beneath an avalanche of associated thoughts and visual images.

An example of how much we invest in the realm of thought is evident in our relationship to the sense of touch. For instance, when the hand reaches out to touch a sexual partner, it is considered a pleasant sensation. But, when the hand touches a pile of garbage, it is considered an unpleasant sensation. Or, if it touches a wall, it may be considered an indifferent sensation. But all that is happening is pressure on the fingertips; the rest is all conceptual thought-forms projected by desire and conditioning.

Most of our world is mind-spin. The power of wisdom is to wake us to the direct experience of things as they are. It dispels our drowsy blindness and allows us to live more of our life, rather then just experiencing the world from the conceptual realm where what we call reality is a dream and a shadow of a dream.

3

Wanting Mind

At the base of the conditioned mind is a wanting. This wanting takes many forms. It wants to be secure. It wants to be happy. It wants to survive. It wants to be loved. It also has specific wants: objects of desire, friendships, food, this color or that color, this kind of surrounding or some other kind. There's wanting not to have pain. There's wanting to be enlightened. There's wanting things to be as we wish they were.

Our daydreams are imaginings of getting what we want; nightmares of being blocked from what we want. The planning mind tries to assure satisfaction. Most thought is based on the satisfaction of desires. Therefore, much thought has at its root a dissatisfaction with what is. Wanting is the urge for the next moment to contain what this moment does not. When there's wanting in the mind, that moment feels incomplete. Wanting is seeking elsewhere. Completeness is being right here.

When we see the depth of wanting in the mind, we see the depth of dissatisfaction because wanting can't be satisfied: when we get finished with one desire there's always another. As long as we're trying to satisfy desire, we're increasing wanting.

Ironically, when we experience the depth of dissatisfaction in the wanting mind there follows a great joy. Because when we see that no object of mind can in itself satisfy, then nothing that arises can draw us out and we begin to let go because there is nothing worth holding onto. The more we see *how* the mind wants, the more we see how wanting obscures the present. To realize that there is nothing to hold onto that can offer lasting satisfaction shows us there is nowhere to go and nothing to have and nothing to be—and that's freedom.

When I first heard the Buddhist ideas about suffering, I strongly resented and resisted them. I thought it was a pessimistic trip. I thought, "Oh this is Buddhist stuff from the East, where half the children die before they're five years old. Of course they think the world's full of suffering, people are starving all around them and lying dead in the streets. But we're not suffering here! I'm not suffering, damn it!" But seeing the scope of my wanting showed me how deeply and subtly dissatisfaction created my personal world, and that seeing freed me from much grasping, from thinking that all my wants had to be satisfied, that I had to compulsively respond to everything that arose in my mind. I saw that things can be a certain way without needing to be acted on or judged or even pushed aside. They can simply be observed.

When I saw how vast, how potent desire is in the mind, I became frightened. I thought there was no way out, not realizing that the power by which I had recognized this condition of suffering was itself the way out. Gradually, seeing the dissatisfactory nature of much of the content of mind was opening a path to freedom. When we see that what we're grasping is on fire, we stop reaching for it. Slowly, the mind is reconditioned to see what it's doing.

And we discover there are many ways that desires cause this dissatisfaction. There are, for instance, things we want that may never come our way, or things we only get once in a while, or which don't stay for long. There are also things we get, and, after we get them, we don't want—which is really disconcerting. Sometimes I see this with my children. They will want something so badly that we'll go from store to store until we find it. Then, we get it and an hour later they're saying, "I wish I hadn't gotten this . . . I wanted the blue one." That's really the heartbreaker. And, that's in all of us. We want and we want and we want . . . and nothing can permanently satisfy us because not only does the thing we want change, but our wants change too. Everything is changing all the time.

Can we think of any pain in our life that was not caused by change? But when we deeply experience this flux we don't recoil in fear of what might be coming but rather begin to open to how things are. We don't get lost in fatalistic imaginings or "nothing matters" nihilism, but instead recognize that everything matters equally.

When the wanting becomes the object of observation, we watch with a clear attention that isn't colored by judgment or choice; it is simply bare attention with nothing added: an openness to receive things as they are. We see that wanting is an automatic, conditioned urge in the mind. And we watch without judging ourselves for wanting. We don't impatiently want to be rid of wanting. We simply observe it.

Only that bare attention, that non-wantingness that can

just be in the moment, has the power to decondition our compulsive reaction to wanting. It disconnects the intense pull of conditioning toward satisfying its wants. Each moment of non-wanting is a moment of freedom. Mindfulness allows that non-wanting. When there is just clear attention, when there is just watching, there's not wanting. If you're watching desire, wanting doesn't continue to seek the object of satisfaction, wanting itself becomes the object of attention and the momentum that leads to action is absorbed.

When we come to see what is freeing and what is not, we come to appreciate what will create more grasping, more painful wanting, and what will take us to wisdom and set us free.

As this practice matures, we come to trust ourselves more. Buddha spoke about these teachings as being "open-handed." The nature of these teachings is "come taste for yourself; it's for all to see." Experience it for yourself. We practice not because we like the teacher or the appealing way the teachings are offered or the people who are practicing the teachings, or even because we admire someone who seems to be working with the method. When we taste it for ourselves, that taste of freedom convinces us.

4

Uncovering Mind

Awareness knows what's going on while it's going on. Concentration has the ability to direct that awareness, to make it one-pointed. Both these qualities are present to some degree in all of us.

When we read a book, as we go from word to word, it's the quality of concentration that allows us to direct our attention to the page. Meanwhile, it's the faculty of awareness that allows understanding of the words as they are read. We've all experienced the feeling when one or the other of these mental factors was absent. If we're tired, sometimes we can read a paragraph over and over and still not understand a word of it. We could even read it out loud and have no idea what it said. There was sufficient concentration to keep the eyes on the page and the reading process going, but there was no awareness of what was going on. On the other hand, if we had awareness but little concentration, we'd be aware of what we were reading, but after a sentence or two we'd slide off into reverie. We wouldn't be able to stay with what we're doing.

Balance

Meditation is the balance of awareness, concentration, and energy. When one predominates over the others, there's an imbalance. Too much energy, and we spin out on thoughts and there may be agitation in the mind. Too much concentration without sufficient energy and the mind dreams off, goes into the half-images of the under-conscious, or dulls into "sinking mind." When awareness is present but energy and concentration are weak, understanding stays superficial; awareness doesn't penetrate, doesn't get to the root of what's occurring in the mind.

It's like working with a magnifying glass: with some objects we want to put the magnifying glass closer and pull the eye back for a longer focus; at other times, the magnifying glass will be placed closer to the eye and farther from the object that's being examined. The magnifying glass is the focus of awareness; the changing requirements of the eyes are like the varying factors of concentration and energy in the mind. It's a moment-to-moment balancing of givens so that observation may occur without strain or laxity, without extremes of any sort, allowing just an easy, balanced awareness of what is happening as it happens. Not a forced stare or a clever squint—just clear-eyed observation of the process as it occurs.

Posture

The posture most people use for meditation is the sitting posture. Sitting on a padded mat with a pillow or *zafu* under the rump will allow the knees to settle more easily to the floor and give a stable base on which to rest. It's difficult at first to get the legs flat on the floor if they're not used to being there. The pillow will help the knees go down, but, more important, as the rump is raised a bit, the back gets straighter. There is no particular merit created by sitting in some eccentric yogic posture. If necessary, we can even sit straight in a chair with our hands in our lap and both feet on the floor.

When we're beginning to meditate, it is advisable not to sit up against a wall or lean back in a chair because there is a tendency to use the wall or chair for support; part of what meditation is, at many levels, is self-support. It is important to feel the body. The tendency to fall asleep is greater when we lean up against something. Even when sitting straight, as the mind stills some, there may be the thought, "Oh, quiet time, must be time for sleep."

Energy comes from exerting energy. When we are attempting to awaken by taking responsibility for our body by sitting, the energy will come, it will be there.

Once we've settled down in the body, attention is brought to focus on a single object to develop the strength of concentration. The object chosen to cultivate this quality of mind is called the primary object. It gives the attention something to come to, to focus on. The natural activity of mind is to wander. It's like a monkey swinging from tree to tree, from thought to thought. Once it gets going, it just goes. Thoughts think themselves. If we imagine that we are the mind, we can just let go of what we're doing and tell the mind to stop—"Okay, mind, stop!" The mind will say, "Okay, I'll stop. Now, just watch me. Here I go . . . there, I stopped! Or, did I? Who's saying all this stuff? Oops, it's me, still." The mind will just go on and on because that's what the mind does. If we identify all these thoughts as "me," then we say we're the mind and we miss the greater part of who we really are. So, we watch the mind as a means of seeing beyond it.

Mindfulness of Breathing

To develop this mindfulness, concentration is cultivated on the primary object of the breath; not the thought of the breath, but a keen and constant awareness of the *sensation* of the breath. It is the sense of touch toward which the attention is directed.

There are two main areas where the sensation of the breath is most noticeable. It is best to choose one and stay with it. The touch of the breath can readily be felt at the nostrils. This is the first of the objects of concentration to choose from. If it is selected, we don't follow it in and out; we simply stay at one point, chosen near the tip of the nose or at the nostrils, wherever the sensation is most noticeable, and note the sensation of breath as it passes. We choose a point of contact and station awareness at that spot and observe from there. It's not a mental picture, it's the physical sensation. We can feel it go in, we can feel it go out. We open our awareness to focus on the experience of the sensation and encourage the return of awareness to that spot.

The awareness of the sensations accompanying each breath becomes the foreground of attention. Though thoughts and other sensations may arise in the background, no energy is needed to displace or act on them. They come and go as they will. If they draw the attention away from the breath, the gentle perseverance of returning

to the breath both strengthens concentration and cultivates the ability of letting go.

The other area where the coming and going of the breath
is quite noticeable is at the point where the abdomen rises
and falls. Attention observes the sensation of the rising and
falling as it occurs of itself with each new breath. The
breath will get subtle, but we watch it as it is; we needn't
do anything. This isn't a breathing exercise, it's an awareness exercise.

After sitting awhile, we may find ourselves thinking the
other point of observation will be easier. It's the "grass is
greener" syndrome, but the grass is exactly the color it is,
just as scintillating or imaginary in one spot as in another.
Going from one spot to another is like digging several
shallow holes for a well. If we want to hit water, we dig
straight down in one place. It's a fascinating process. There
really is no goal except knowing what's happening right
now.

Noting

To aid in the early stages of practice, we may want to
mentally note "in" with each in breath at the nostrils and
"out" with each out breath or "rising/falling" if observation
has been established at the abdomen. Noting can be a very
useful tool to keep us awake to the process of the present
moment, such as noting "thinking, thinking" when thought
intrudes, or "smelling, smelling" when a whiff of perfume
is perceived or "hearing, hearing" when a car goes by. Noting is a technique which keeps us on the track.

Noting keeps the attention close to the object of awareness. Noting is not a comment on what's happening, it is a simple recognition of what is occurring, without comment or judgment of any sort. It's done with an easy, spacious recognition that does not depend on the language used, which is only employed to keep the mind alert to its own process.

"Thinking, thinking" may suffice to acknowledge the thought process as it predominates, though at times a more precise acknowledgment will be useful in uncovering the subtleties of the thinking mind, such as "planning, planning" when the planning mind occurs, or "fear, fear" when a mind of fear arises.

These notings can keep the awareness of what is happening in the moment sharp and clear. However, it may well be the case that, as concentration deepens, the process of noting might become an interference, a tool that is not of much value any longer. As awareness penetrates, it may not need to note to maintain a keen alertness of the objects present. Then, noting may naturally fall away or be let go.

The usefulness of noting may also vary from day to day at some stages of concentration and awareness. At times, it may be useful until concentration deepens and then become unnecessary. Or we may notice that the awareness is generally clear and on the object until it gets lost into certain states of mind that arise repeatedly; so, noting might be used just to identify those states which still cause identification and thus draw away attention. Fear or lusty daydreaming are two particular examples that might necessitate the conscious recollection that noting provides.

Noting allows us to gently, but perseveringly, stay with our experience, acknowledging whatever predominates as it arises. When attention wanders, as it's used to, we recognize the wandering and gently return it to the breath. We don't try to tough-off the mind, to force it to its object. Force creates a stiffness in the mind, a kind of goal-orientation that wishes for things to be otherwise, which is pushing against the moment, trying to break into the future. It is a cumbersome mind, a mind very full of self and *doing*.

Sensation

Many sensations may be noted as awareness deepens. When we get messages from the body, we just listen to them. If we feel discomfort, we just note it as "discomfort," not getting tough with it, not getting rigid. If there's pain, we relax around it, and note it as "pain, pain," or some such words natural to our feeling. It's best not to move about, noticing the urge to move, the urge to escape discomfort; allow the body to just sit. The stiller the body, the stiller the mind.

When we're attending to sensation, either with each breath or as feelings in the body, we're not at the level where words are produced. We're breaking the internal dialogue, the constant comment of mind, breaking through that place where thinking occurs and directly experiencing the process. It is this kind of direct experience which opens the intuition and insight of the wisdom mind, which brings the mind face to face with itself.

Thought

Thoughts are mental objects. They can be seen passing like bubbles through the field of awareness. Thought is usually formulated in words, but a thought can be a visual image or even some remembered sense impression before it breaks into a galloping fantasy. In observing thoughts, it is important not to comment or judge their content, but only to see them clearly as they arise. Thinking about thinking is not meditation.

When we're watching the breath and thinking occurs, we can note "thinking, thinking" and come back to noting the breath. But the pull of mental objects can be very strong and subtle, and the mind skates off into "Oh, I'm doing pretty well—ah, caught myself—thinking, thinking—rising, falling, rising, falling—well, caught it that time, didn't I?—oh oh, blew it again!—thinking, thinking—rising, falling, rising falling—Well, so far, so good—wow, there I go again, can't I stay on the breath even a minute! What a clod I am—oops, there's judging again—hey, I'm lost, which way to the breath?" Just note "thinking, thinking" and come back to the breath again. Stay simple and easy.

At times, there may be extremely attractive thought forms while we are meditating: good ideas, beautiful images, great inventions. These objects of mind need not be distractions; indeed, if clearly seen, nothing becomes a distraction. It is all just seen as part of the mindflow, full of karma and interesting trinkets. Just note those things and come back easily into the breath. Indeed, coming back to the breath helps us discover the power of letting go and deepens our ability to relinquish mind's conditioned grasping. There is no need to worry that a good idea or the solution to an old problem will be lost; what is of value will be available at the proper moment.

The deepening of concentration is a natural process,

like the capacity of a muscle to strengthen with continued usage. Every time we return to the breath, our concentration gets stronger. Mind may view this and judge, "I'm doing better," which, if not recognized as a thought, becomes a distracted mind creating more self and being less concentrated in the doing. Letting go of "knowing" allows us to directly experience how things are.

Attachment makes us want to encourage some images or feelings and push others away: to *do* something about them. Attachment means we're identifying with those ideas or sensations. But, as long as we're identifying with anything that's coming up, thinking it is "me" or "mine," we won't see how it comes, we won't see the process out of which it arises. As long as we're identifying with content, we're not really free. The difference between being in bondage and being liberated is the difference between thinking and recognizing thought as thought.

Volition

Normally, we scratch without realizing that we itch. Our actions arise beyond awareness of what motivates them. But the volitional element of mind, that quality we often refer to as will or intention, can be clearly perceived when mind is silent and aware. We are constantly changing position as we speak or read or eat, not noticing that we are reacting to some discomfiture, that we are being moved by mind, unaware of the intention to be rid of some stiffness in the neck or an ache in the legs. We are moved again and again by the mind's aversions and attractions, seldom noticing the intention which activates the body's movements. We are often like robots; moved, but unknowing.

Volition is part of the ongoing message which allows us to walk by making one foot follow the other, it can be seen as the subtle, preverbal urge that makes us duck when a rock hits the windshield. But even these subtle urges can be observed almost like sensations in the mind. Volition can also be a good deal more evident, such as when we are passing an ice cream store, the thought occurs "I'll just have a single-dip butter pecan," the voice of volitional mind, the predecessor of all karma.

By observing the intention which precedes voluntary activity, we begin to dethrone the power of desire to unconsciously condition our actions, and we gain a bit more freedom in our lives. Before each word or gesture, intention subtly precedes the activity; this transmits the energy from wanting to doing. Just as the volitional element can be noticed leading to further and further spinnings and longings of the mind, so, too, can it be seen that it is this quality of choice which returns us again and again to the breath that, rightly encouraged, balances life.

States of Mind

A state of mind is an attitude, a predominant emotion or mood, that acts like a filter or colored lens through which mental objects such as thoughts and sensations are experienced and related to. States of mind are ways of seeing. We can experience a complete set of attitudes and emotions pass away and a whole new mind quite different in its perspective come into existence immediately thereafter.

Over and over, these states of mind arise with a seemingly wholly independent life of their own, only to be replaced by the next mind state that enters stage left. Each of these minds is adroitly adhered to as "I," "me," "mine," though they may differ drastically in character and intention. Indeed, any object or thought that enters the field of awareness may alternately be liked or disliked in alternating mind moments.

We contain conflicting desire systems that may push an object away one moment and grasp at it the next. These conflicting desire systems may want to do something at one time, but not at another. These conflicting mind states and their concomitant judging of each other cause much of the friction that we experience as guilt. One mind arises to be naturally followed by another. To identify with one quality or mood and disallow the other is to deny the flow and become trapped in the painful backwash of the mind.

At one moment the state of mind might be joyful or alert or happy or kind, while at another it might be angry or greedy or lusty or slothful. Indeed, it vacillates a thousand times a day between these various states. Because of the changing nature of mind states, some people try to control the mind. But it is more important, I think, not to allow the mind to control us. Some people imagine that meditation is stopping the mind. Though it might be done for a short period, it does not decrease the sense of attachment to mind; indeed, by there being "someone" accomplishing something, it may even increase the "I" illusion. Stopping the mind does not bring wisdom; what brings wisdom is understanding the nature of mind. With that understanding comes a shedding of identification with the mind and an opportunity to become free.

Choiceless Awareness

No object is any better to observe than any other. The ideal object is precisely what is happening in the moment. When we watch the mind with what is called "choiceless awareness," we take the concentration that developed on the primary object and allow it, moment to moment, to experience anything that arises; whatever becomes predominant is seen with an awareness that does not cling. We are just choicelessly watching whatever is happening. There is no judgment in that openness of mind. It does not prefer any object to any other. And that is both the goal and the method; the beauty of this meditation. Every moment of practice is also the goal of the practice: mindfulness, simply being awake to what is.

When mindfulness becomes very keen we can begin to see thoughts in a new way, literally experiencing them arising and passing away as though they had a frame around them. It's as though we'd taken a movie film, which we had been watching projected on a screen, and examined it frame by frame, investigating the discrete elements of what had previously been imagined to be a single, continuous flow. We see the arising and passing away of consciousness, of everything that we considered to be self. It allows a microscopic examination of moment-to-moment mind, of being, as it unfolds. Then, what is unconscious becomes conscious. Nothing is blocked and nothing is added, the whole universe presents itself as it will and we are graced to perceive it.

It's like standing on a stream bank, watching all the thoughts float downstream like bubbles. And, as we watch, it becomes increasingly clear that some of the bubbles are us watching the stream, that even the watcher is just part of the flow, and awareness simply experiences all that is.

A Train of Thought

An image about practicing meditation that may be helpful is that of standing at a railroad crossing, watching a freight train passing by. In each transparent boxcar, there is a thought. We try to look straight ahead into the present, but our attachments draw our attention into the contents of the passing boxcars: we identify with the various thoughts. As we attend to the train, we notice there's supper in one boxcar, but we just ate, so we're not pulled by that one. The laundry list is the next one, so we reflect for a moment on the blue towel hanging on the line to dry, but we wake up quite quickly to the present once again, as the next boxcar has someone in it meditating and we recall what we're doing. A few more boxcars go by with thoughts clearly recognized as thoughts. But, in the next one is a snarling lion chasing someone who looks like us. We stay with that one until it's way down the line to see if it got us. We identify with that one because it "means" something to us. We have an attachment to it. Then we notice we've missed all the other boxcars streaming by in the meantime and we let go of our fascination for the lion and bring our attention straight ahead into the present once again.

We stick to some and we don't stick to others. The train is just there—and the silent witness who's standing at the crossroads also seems to be there. Those are the first stages of trying to be mindful, trying to stay in the here and now.

Then, as we're a bit more used to being aware of the contents, we start noticing the process of the train going by—just boxcar after boxcar—and our attention doesn't follow every stimulus: we don't keep getting lost down the track in the past or anticipating what's coming from the future. So, we're looking straight ahead, not distracted by any of the contents, when all of a sudden one of the boxcars explodes as it goes by. We're drawn out into that one, we jump into the action in that boxcar. Then we come back with a wry smile full of recognition that it was just an image of an explosion, just a boxcar thought. And, again, we are straight ahead with just the process of passing boxcars, when there we are beating our wife in one of the boxcars. There's all kinds of stuff in the mind. And we're going to follow it, to be pulled by it, until we start seeing the impersonal, conditioned nature of the contents and recognize the perfect flow of the process itself.

Then, we notice as we look straight ahead that we're starting to be able to see between the cars. And we begin to see what's on the other side of the train, what is beyond thought. We experience that the process is occurring against a background of undifferentiated openness, that, moment to moment, mind is arising and passing away in vast space.

As we experience the frame of reference in which all this melodrama is occurring, it begins freeing us from being so carried away—even by fear. We start seeing. "Ah, there's the exploding boxcar trick again," or "There's the angry boss one again." Whatever it is, we start seeing it as part of the process. We see it in context. The small mind that identifies with all that stuff starts becoming bigger and bigger and bigger, starts encompassing even itself in a mind so vast it has room for everything and everyone, including the train and the observer. And, then, even that fellow standing at the crossroads watching turns out to be just the contents of one of those boxcars, just another object of mind. And awareness, standing nowhere, is everywhere at once.

5

A Guided Meditation on Mindfulness (Vipassana)

(To be fed slowly to oneself or read aloud to a friend.)

Find a comfortable place to sit, with the back straight, but not rigid.

Allowing the body to just breath naturally, bring the attention to the most noticeable point of touch where the breath makes contact as it enters the nostrils.

Bring the awareness to the sense of touch of the air as it passes in and passes out. Station the attention like a watchman at a city gate who notices those passing in and passing out, but does not follow them in or out—who just stays alert at the gate.

Keep your attention at one precise point and note the sensation that accompanies each breath as it flows in and flows out of the body in the natural breathing process.

If the attention strays, bring it back to the touching point that notices the breath as it comes and goes at the nostrils. Noting "breathing in; breathing out." Not thinking about the breath. Not even visualizing it. Just being with the sensation as it arises with the touch of the air passing in and out of the nostrils.

Sounds arise. Thoughts arise. Other sensations arise. All background, arising and passing away.

In the foreground is the moment-to-moment awareness of the sensation of the breath coming and going. Not pushing anything away. Not grasping at anything. Just clear, precise, gentle observation of the breath. Mindfulness of breathing.

Sensations arise in the body. Thoughts arise in the mind. They come and go like bubbles.

Each mind moment is allowed to arise and allowed to pass away of its own momentum. No pushing away of the mind, no grasping at the breath. Just gently returning awareness to the sensations always present with the coming and going of the breath. Gently returning.

The awareness of breath is foreground. In the background, everything else is as it is, but the open, soft mind doesn't stick.

Each breath unique: sometimes deep, sometimes shallow, always slightly changing. The whole breath felt going in, stopping, and coming out; the whole breath experienced at the level of sensation, of touch.

Breathing just happening by itself. Awareness simply watching. The whole body relaxed. Eyes soft. Face relaxed. Shoulders loose. The belly full and easy. No holding anywhere. Just awareness and breathing.

Just consciousness and the object of consciousness, arising and passing away moment to moment in the vast space of mind.

Don't get lost. If the mind pulls away, gently, with a soft, non-judging, non-clinging awareness, return to the breath. Note the whole breath, from its beginning to its end, precisely, clearly, from sensation to sensation.

The body breathes by itself. The mind thinks by itself. Awareness simply observes the process without getting lost in the content.

Each breath unique. Each moment completely new.

If sensation should arise in the body, let the awareness recognize it as sensation. Notice it coming and notice it going. Not thinking of it as body or as leg, as pain or as vibration. Simply noting it as sensation and returning to the breath.

The whole process occurring by itself. Awareness observing, moment to moment, the arising and passing away of experiences in the mind and body. Moment-to-moment change.

In the foreground, awareness of the sensation of breathing as it comes and goes by itself. Just breath, and awareness of breath.

Surrender to the breath. Experience the breath. Don't try to get anything from the breath. Don't even think of concentration. Just allow awareness to penetrate to the level of sensations that arise of themselves and by themselves.

The point of touch becoming more and more distinct, more intense with the coming and going of each breath.

The mind becoming one-pointed on the sensations that accompany breathing.

If thoughts arise, clearly note their motion in mind, rising and passing away like bubbles. Notice them, and return to the mindfulness of the breathing.

If thought or feeling becomes predominant, with an open awareness, softly note what is predominant as "feeling" or "thinking," as "hearing," as "tasting," as "smelling." Then, gently return to the breath.

Don't tarry with thought. Don't identify contents. Just

note the experience of thought entering and passing away, of feeling, of any sense, arising in the moment and passing away in the next moment.

Return to the even flow of the breath. Not grasping at anything. Not pushing anything away. Just a clear awareness of what predominates in the mind or body as it arises.

Returning deeply to the intense point of sensation that marks the passage of the air of each full breath.

The eyes soft. Shoulders soft. Belly soft. The awareness crystal clear.

Subtler and subtler sensations become predominant. Thoughts become predominant. Each one noted clearly within the concentrated awareness of breathing.

Watch its motion, continual change from object to object, breath to breath, sensation to sensation. Like a kaleidoscope, continual change.

Moment-to-moment objects arise and pass away in the vast space of mind, of body. An easy, open awareness simply observing the process of arising and passing away. Awareness of whatever is predominant, returning to the sensations of the breath.

Feelings arise. Thoughts arise. The "planning mind," the "judging mind." Awareness experiences the process of their movement. It doesn't get lost in content. Observe thought passing through the vast space of mind.

These words arising from nothing, disappearing into nothing. Just open space in which the whole mind, the whole body, are experienced as moment-to-moment change.

Sound arises and passes away.

Feeling arises and passes away.

All of who we are, of what we think we are, moment to moment, coming and going, bubbles in mind, arising and *passing away in the vast, open space of mind. Choiceless awareness. Moment-to-moment awareness of whatever arises, of whatever exists.*

All things which have the nature to arise have the nature to pass away. Everything we think of as "me" disappearing moment to moment.

Moment to moment, just seeing it all as it is, perfectly coming and going of itself.

"Thus shall ye think of all this fleeting world: a star at dawn, a bubble in a stream, a flash of lightning in a summer cloud, a flickering lamp, a phantom and a dream."

6

Self Image and the Imagined Self

It's very seldom that we go through a day or even an hour in which there aren't states of mind that we wish we didn't experience—feelings of self-consciousness, tension, anger, aversion, fear, envy, tiredness. It's also common that, in the course of a day, quite attractive, pleasant states of mind arise that we wish we had more often, that we want to last forever. Somehow, some corner of the mind wants to convince itself that we are only the pleasant states. That's just selective identification, attachment, clinging to some self image, some way we wish to see ourselves.

Moment to moment, the mind, the conditioning, is building some image of who it thinks it is. We think we're the beautiful, pleasant states; we don't want to be depression, anger, agitation, grief, frustration. We're attached to one aspect as opposed to another and, therefore, fail to see the process out of which it's all coming.

But it's very difficult to see what's real when we're actively filtering all the input, when there is "someone" in there trying to be something. The "I" is reconstructed moment to moment out of our liking and disliking of what is happening in the mind. This acquired judgment of each

thing which comes to mind picks and chooses among multiple thoughts and images to construct its house, which is
constantly dissolving in the natural flow of mind. This
"I" is the façade chosen by mind to represent it. When
choosing who we wish we were, we cull from the great
mix an image here and there, and discredit the rest through
some rationalization. What we choose, or what is allowed
to remain, we call "I"—believing all the while that this "I"
is choosing rather than what actually has been chosen.
Thus the imaginary "I" is continually engaged in the compulsive activity of reforming itself. But this separate "I,"
this aspect of mind which chooses among its own images
for something to be, is just more mind, just another passing thought, a bubble.

We're constantly building a new image of ourselves and
wondering what's next. We have allowed ourselves very little space for not-knowing. Very seldom do we have the wisdom not-to-know, to lay the mind open to deeper understanding. When confusion occurs in the mind, we identify
with it and say we are confused: we hold onto it. Confusion
arises because we fight against our not-knowing, which experiences each moment afresh without preconceptions or
expectations. We are so full of ways of seeing and ideas of
how things should be we leave no room for wisdom to
arise. We desire to know in only a certain way, a way which
will corroborate our image of a rational, separate, auton-
omous self. When we open our minds, our hearts, not *trying* to understand, but simply allowing understanding to
occur, we find more than was expected. When we let go of
our ignorance and confusion, we allow our knowing mind
to arise.

Wisdom occurs in the mind that rests in not knowing,

the still mind that simply is. There's nothing that is absent from our being which a Buddha or a Christ or a Mohammed possesses; it is the same wellspring, the same original nature, a shared essence. In letting go of who we imagine ourselves to be, letting go of our thinking, our attempt to control the world, we come upon our natural being which has been waiting patiently all these years for us to come home.

By clinging to what we think we know or don't know, we block our deeper knowing. By gently letting go of everything—not through force, not by slaying it, but simply seeing all the content as passing show, as process and flow—we become the whole of our experience and open to our natural understanding.

It might be useful to further define "letting go." Letting go means not dwelling on something which has come to mind. It also means experiencing that quality of non-grasping awareness which pulls nothing from the flow—experiencing a great spaciousness which simply lets everything come and lets everything go.

This spaciousness is better understood when we notice that usually the mind closes down on each thought. The mind takes on the shape of each object that comes into it. The mind thinks of an apple, it becomes an apple. It thinks of fear, it becomes fear. Therefore we have come to believe that mind is the contents of the mind. But the mind is no more the contents of the mind than the sky is the clouds which pass through it. The mind is a space in which these contents are occurring, are arising and passing away. The experience of this spaciousness is the essence of non-grasping, of letting go, of having room for everything and holding to nothing.

When we relate to this open space instead of its contents, we're not tightening down on anything passing through. If fear or wanting arises, it is seen within the spaciousness that surrounds it. We don't get lost by becoming it, but simply see it as just another moment in the mind flow, another something which arose uninvited and will pass away in the same manner.

By letting go of all we believe we are, by letting go of thinking we're the body or the mind, that we're brilliant or stupid, a saint or a fool, we at last become whole again and awaken to the universe within us. If we let go of everything, we can have anything. But if we hold anything at all, we lose everything else and that thing we cling to eventually must change and become a cause for pain.

To develop a mind that clings to nothing is the path to wisdom. Thoughts arise, sensations are felt, the senses are open and received, there are preferences and opinions arising in the spaciousness of mind; but seen clearly there is no identification or interference.

So we see that in the spaciousness of letting go there arises a natural balance. By our letting go of confusion, knowing arises. By our letting go of anger, love arises. We don't have to import love, we need only let go of that which blocks it. By our letting go of fear, calm arises. Love and peacefulness, care and generosity are all natural qualities of being that are evident when not blocked by mental traits acquired to preserve and express the imagined self.

In the stillness of meditation practice, these obstructive states are more easily seen and released, but during the day it's not so easy. We become forgetful and drop back into our conditioned beliefs and identifications. We wonder how we can uproot the confusion which starts an argument, or get rid of anger at the boss, or boredom or restlessness on the job. In our daily lives we discover that by using the same technique of just acknowledging the state of mind as we did during meditation, by just naming it and giving it space—"Ah, there's anger again," or, "Well, that feels like a bit of fear coming up"—we bring it out into the light of awareness and it loses its great power over us. Even if we acknowledged our state of mind once an hour, this practice of noting what happens as it occurs would decrease the intensity of identification with these states and allow a greater spaciousness to the whole day. During the day, if we acknowledge the fear or the dullness, we cut through it. Each time we acknowledge a state of mind without judgment, just noting, "There's insecurity," or, "There's fear," or "Well, look at that restlessness," it weakens the state of mind while strengthening the ability to let it go.

As the negative states weaken, the positive states arise of and by themselves. Such terms as "negative" and "positive," or "unwholesome" and "wholesome," are not meant judgmentally. Rather, they indicate those states that block the light of understanding and those which focus it. We easily recognize negative states: they are uncomfortable, we can feel them in our body. What does it feel like to be angry or jealous or envious? It feels tight and anxious, there is a burning. What does it feel like to be generous, open, kind, loving? It feels warm and spacious, it feels very comfortable.

Seeing what's happening, even if it's unpleasant to acknowledge, can feel very good because it's the truth of the moment and the truth is beautiful. Even acknowledging "I feel uptight" openly in a spacious, non-judgmental manner, frees the tightness and the fear which maintain it, and can unblock the heart by its self-acceptance. Trying to hide from the negative states, to distract ourselves or run away, just invites them to come back because of the negative attachment. It just tightens the knots. The spaciousness that allows everything to be as it is, allows the tensions to unravel themselves, lets go of the pain of resistance.

We seldom recognize our state of mind because we're so identified with it most of the time. We don't have the space between the attention and the feeling to see it is not us, to remember to simply acknowledge it. We don't usually even recognize how deeply we're identified with a mood or state of mind because we're seeing the whole world from inside it. We're judging and commenting on everything from that point of view, the self image of the moment, the happy "me" with its predilections, or the bored "me" with its desires. We become the states of mind instead of allowing them to just pass through awareness without sticking to them. By encouraging this spacious non-identifying awareness we let go of being anyone at all trying to get anything at all—we don't hold back the flow, or push it; we just allow it all to pass as it does.

7

Judging Mind

The judging mind has an opinion about everything. It selects from the mindflow who it believes it ought to be and chides the rest. It's full of noise and old learning. It is a quality of mind addicted to maintaining an image of itself. It is always trying to be somebody.

Judging mind oversees the process of all our thoughts and actions with a constant nagging prattle. It is one of the voices of the internal dialogue which supports what we suppose is the "ego." When there's judgment, there is "someone" judging, there is an "I am" embroiled in the dance identified with phenomena as "me," someone quite separate from the flow, the process. All of the "yes/no's" in our life have contributed to its power, all the good/bads, all the right/wrongs, all the conflicting ideas of how things "should" be. It is a fierce and constant critic of all that comes within the mind. But, because it is just another process of the mind, it can be brought into the light of understanding and let go of.

Sometimes when we're meditating and get drawn into thought, we have a tendency to think, "Darn it, I'm lost thinking again"; to follow a wandering thought with the habitual judging comment; and then as we recognize our judgment to react with, "Damn it, there I am judging again." We judge the judging mind.

When judging arises, if we acknowledge it with a spacious, non-judgmental attention, we loosen its grasp by seeing it with compassion for the process that we are, with a respectful recognition of the enormity of the power of conditioning to draw us out. We're going to get lost thousands and thousands of times. But letting go of who we think we are, instead of judging it, allows our life to soften. Identification with thought solicits judgment. If we are simply aware that the mind is judging when it's judging, and acknowledge it with open, clear attention, the judging mind begins to dissolve.

But the mind that comments on itself with the tightness of judgment doesn't allow for the spaciousness which has room for the whole being. Spaciousness bids nothing come and bids nothing stay, it just allows for the nature of mind.

To maintain the spaciousness which can non-judgmentally acknowledge the judging mind requires a balancing act. If we're too close to any thought or state of mind—if we're right on top of it—there's a pressure, a tightness, which does not allow the natural flow the space it needs to be seen in its totality. It's like pressing your face against the plate glass to see something in a shop window. We distort our vision, just as standing too far back from the window causes the objects to be indistinct. If we're too close, we can't focus; if we're too distant, we aren't alert to subtle detail. The balancing comes from investigating how we are seeing. The subtle adjustments come from trusting the intuitive wisdom of the process.

When the judging mind is clearly noted, its fragile nature

can be observed. We see opinions forming and melting away like snowflakes. We see that each comment is like a bubble. When awareness touches it, its insubstantiality, its essential emptiness, becomes readily apparent. The likes and dislikes of the judging mind are just old karma and conditioning running off. But if we compulsively react to these preferences, if we identify with them, they become the cause of new karma. Judging can be very subtle; a single moment of praise or blame, of liking or disliking polarizes our whole world. This automatic clinging and condemning of the judging mind is an ongoing karmic flow that need not be the motivator of new karma-creating action. A moment of judgmental mind, a mind lost in identification with old preferences, is a moment of forgetfulness, of ignorance. A moment of recognition of judgmental mind is a moment of freedom and wisdom.

Someone asked, "How can we maintain if we don't judge? Aren't we then completely indiscriminate?" That question comes from a basic lack of trust of ourselves, a disbelief that if we really let go we'll be okay. Some people believe that if we let go of our constant judgmental overseer we'll become wild, rabid beasts; if we're not constantly under control, constantly suppressing this thought or that thought, constantly manipulating the mind, we'll run rampant and cause harm. We don't realize that when the mind is soft and non-grasping we don't get caught in the melodramas which cause such pain to ourselves and to others. We can trust the awareness which allows judging to be seen as just part of the flow, an outcome of previous conditioning that need not direct or limit the spacious mind. The judging mind tries to convince us that we've constantly got to be on top of ourselves, insisting that if we don't, we'll become totally unacceptable to those whose love we want most. But actually our ability to love and be loved is directly equatable to the degree that we are able to let go of our separateness, to let ourselves be loved by letting go of our judgmental self-consciousness.

In some translations of yogic texts, we hear about "mind-control," which tends to make us think that we must hone the judgmental quality to control the mind. But real control is letting go. We're free when we let go because then nothing that arises can pull at us—not anger or greed or fear—because there's nowhere for it to stick.

When we're non-judgmentally observing the mind, we see clearly the difference between thinking and watching thought. Watching thought is letting go of the content as we become aware of the process, seeing the space around each object of the mind. Thinking is diving right into the karma which causes the thought, the object, and reinforcing its activity while strengthening its ability to cause identification and reaction in the future.

Christ said, "Judge not lest ye be judged." The more we exercise the judging mind on others, the more forcefully the judging mind will be encouraged to appraise each of our actions. The best means of defusing the judging mind is simply to non-judgmentally recognize it as it occurs.

A few years ago, I noticed that in public places my mind would often begin judging strangers in the room. It was an automatic, rather annoying process cultivated over years of competing and comparing. It seemed to be a way of maintaining my presence in the room. It was ridiculous, but it was happening much of the time. It was particularly noticeable in restaurants when I would overhear the people in the next booth. I was quite critical of their communication, of who I imagined they thought they were. I noticed how superior I believed I was. The mind was hypnotically running off its judgmental quality.

So I watched and didn't suppress it, I just noticed what it was doing. I watched it insult me and the people next to me in a single swipe. As I worked with this judging quality, I saw how awareness, and a growing sense of cosmic humor cut through this rather sticky mind state and, progressively weakened its authority. I experienced its voice getting weaker and weaker as it lost its potency. Though occasionally I still notice the mind judging conversation from the next booth, it has less pull. I watch it run out its habitual momentum.

There are moments when we'll be free of that inner struggle, and there'll be other moments when the undercurrent of conditioning is so strong that we're drawn back into judging again. When the voice of the judging mind is particularly loud, we are afforded the opportunity to rediscover the power of self-forgiveness. The openness generated by self-forgiveness is so great that it dissipates the tightness of the judging mind. With kindness to ourself we develop compassion for the difficulties that arise during this gradual awakening. We experience a deep respect for the process we are uncovering and are slowly understanding. We see that to judge ourselves for being as we are is like judging the sky for its weather or the coming and going of the tides. Self-acceptance and spacious awareness allow us to experience our precious life as it is without judgmental divisiveness. To be kind and awake to ourselves and let go of even the sense of unworthiness opens us to our wholeness.

8

The Sense of Unworthiness

The person we want most to love us is ourself. But when we attempt to bring love to ourself, perhaps through a meditation in which we cultivate this quality or in the course of our most ordinary day, we discover that we sometimes think we don't deserve it. We see self-doubt arising to block this love, an interference which we realize is usually present to some degree almost all of the time. It is a sense of unworthiness that we carry with us like a cloud. It blinds us to our beauty. I see in some of the most beautiful beings I know that the hottest fire they have to work with is their sense of unworthiness.

That sense of unworthiness, it seems, comes out of our being talked out of, trained out of, conditioned out of trusting our natural being. It is the result of being turned away from ourselves, taught to distrust ourselves. An oversimplified example is that as children, toddling across the floor, we may have had the experience of needing to urinate, so we did. And Mommy or Daddy may have come up and said, "Oh no! That's wrong, don't do that!" But we didn't *do* anything; we just peed. It's just something that naturally came about through us. But, somehow, it was "wrong!" It caused us to increasingly question our naturalness.

As we grow older, we learn to take care of ourselves, to be responsible. We are encouraged to be someone special, to be praiseworthy, to be outstanding. And in the course of learning how to reinforce our separateness, it's quite natural that most of us as children at some time lie or steal. We may lie to protect our "specialness," to suit some image of what we are supposed to be, to disguise our natural waywardness, to be someone we're not, just as sometimes we may steal to feed ourselves what we wish we already had.

The child is told not to lie and not to steal, but never told *how* not to lie and not to steal. Our naturalness is accused. Our distrust in ourselves is reaffirmed by the feeling that we're the only ones who ever lied or ever stole, that there's something basically wrong with us.

There is within us, much of the time, that critical judging voice commenting on what we're doing and how we're doing it, pointing out that we're not coming up to par, not being worthy of love. We have somehow come to think that it's not appropriate to love ourselves—that we're not worthy of self-love—because we have lost our natural love of ourselves, our natural self-respect.

Interestingly enough, it's the sense of unworthiness which maintains ego. We don't have to battle or crush the ego. Much of what we see as ego-motivation comes from a sense of unworthiness. When the sense of unworthiness falls away, there is a good deal less ego support. The ego is not an entity out to conquer the world; much of the momentary grasping we call ego is a compensatory mechanism trying to disprove unworthiness. It's not so much trying to appear great as trying not to seem a fool. Being someone special, we suspect, will compensate for this inadequacy, will show that we are really okay.

When we let go of that unworthiness, when we forgive ourselves for even that, then no one is trying to prove anything. Then the whole ego-structure starts to crumble, and opens itself to much love and self-acceptance. When self-judgment comes up, we try gently to let go of it. The next thought might well be, "Oh, I can't do that, that's self-indulgence. I mustn't let myself get away with that!" which is more of that belief that we have to control ourselves, that we can't trust ourselves. Our feeling of distrust in our natural being has gained such potency, and has been supported by so much of society, that many will agree wholeheartedly that we mustn't trust ourselves.

There is so much distrust in our natural being that many people are convinced that man is by nature evil. That's the sense of unworthiness that we spoke of in relation to the judging mind. People who feel this look at the hindrances in the mind—the greed and the desires, the stuff we all work with, the anger, the selfishness—and say, "Look at that awful stuff. Can I trust a mind that's got all that in it?" But when we suggest that these hindrances are encouraged by such aversion and fear, that one may let go of this conditioned mind and let the natural wisdom arise, they say, "I can't let go of control—I've got to keep the screws on or I'll really blow it." Actually, our sense of unworthiness causes us to reinforce those negative qualities. And, since all of those qualities encourage further separation, it makes us feel even more unloved and unlovable, and makes contact with ourselves and others yet more difficult.

We can note unworthiness just like any other quality of

mind coming and going as it will in response to certain conditions. It's just another moment in mind. It's just another part of the passing show. We can trust ourselves and the power of awareness to penetrate to a clear comprehension of the truth. All our trying to change, thinking we have to *do* something about how and who we are comes mostly from a sense of unworthiness, a sense of personal distrust. Even now a lot of us are saying, "Yes, but . . ." That's just more of the same.

A dear friend, talking to a group about her life, referred to what she called a "cosmic-consciousness experience." She had, a few months before, experienced a wonderful understanding of how things are. As she told the story, somebody in the audience who was a little testy asked, "Are you bragging about having an experience somebody else hasn't had? Are you creating attachment to peak experiences?"

She replied, "No, you know, it wasn't the knowledge that came out of it, or the wisdom, or even the peace. What was really important for me about this experience was that I was worthy to have it."

It's not uncommon for the sense of unworthiness to become more distinct, and seem like it's gotten worse, as awareness deepens and uncovers yet more of its subtle tendencies. Then, it becomes the basis for work on ourselves, for much purification.

We let go of our sense of unworthiness not by submitting it to the ax or trying to control or suppress it, but by giving it enough room to see its own workings.

A sense of unworthiness does not make us unworthy. It's been acquired over many lifetimes—if not billions of mind-moments in this life—when we were told or thought we were wrong or inadequate. Everybody seems to have it to some degree. I don't know if every culture encourages it to the same degree as ours, but it is very prevalent in this society.

We are worthy of letting go of our unworthiness. If we did nothing but practice letting go of unworthiness, much of the stuff we're working so hard to clear away would have no support system. We would have more room to grow.

Consciously we surrender unworthiness as it arises, not entertaining it with the ego's list of credits. The work which will awaken us is that of becoming keenly aware of unworthiness without judging it. Gently, with patience and a lot of love, we acknowledge the being we really are. As a friend puts it, "Always try to see yourself through God's eyes."

9

Self-accepting Mindfulness

The more we accept of ourselves, the more fully we experience the world. The more we accept our anger, our loneliness, our desire systems, the more we can hear others and the more we can hear ourselves. The amount of space that we're still denying is the distance between us and completion. Because completion isn't being anywhere else.

When we can be with whatever is happening in the moment, our sense of completeness will be present. Our feeling of wholeness, of fulfillment, will be present as we open to whatever's happening in the moment. We don't have to *do* anything about it. Doing is usually the desire for something to be otherwise. When we can surrender into the moment without any attachment anywhere, so that anything that arises is seen with a soft, non-judging mind, we experience our completeness. We can be with our loneliness, or our fear, or even our self-consciousness in a very complete way. We see that those are just passing states of mind, and, though they may be painful to acknowledge, the recognition of their presence is the truth and the truth is beautiful. It means really accepting all of what we are.

Only when we accept all of what we are, are we going to see what's behind it.

Anger is a particularly good example of something we don't want to acknowledge in ourselves, something we judge as "bad." But when frustration arises, anger often follows. When we're watching the mind closely, we can see frustration turn to anger. We can observe that unfulfilled wanting all of a sudden flip into anger. We see how a frustration has become an anger, and that often the anger seeks to blame something. The anger is: we want it, we didn't get it, and then the closing of the heart turns into a clenched fist.

Anger's a particularly good state to watch because we've been told not to be angry, and often we've been told not to be angry by someone who's angry. That leaves us with a very strange message. Because there is some anger in most people, somewhere there may be a knot of impotent rage because everything's changing and just beyond our control. As a child, our puppy died or our parents died, or we moved, or our best friend moved. It may sometimes seem as though everything we love will be lost to circumstances. Either it's going to change or die, or we will. Just as with the child who is continually told what to do and constantly encouraged to distrust his most natural direction, there's a deep sense of loss somewhere within and it sometimes creates a deep anger.

When we uncover this knot of fear and anger we are a bit astonished, but until we accept it with genuine loving-kindness for ourselves, until we accept it fully, with a compassion for how human we are, we can't let it go. As long as we're suppressing it, our attachment is nurturing its roots. It's painful to acknowledge our anger. But it's okay to be angry, and it's okay not to be angry, too. It's okay to let it come and let it go. We have to hear how it is for each of us. When I say it's okay to be angry, some people get a little chill: "What do you mean it's okay to be angry? I've been told it's not okay to be angry. It isn't okay to hurt anybody." Anger is a mind state; it takes volition to create the action. If it's seen clearly, it doesn't hurt anybody. It's when we get lost into it that it hurts somebody. And one way we get lost into it is by saying, "I'm not angry!"

Striking out at somebody in anger is not a very creative or wholesome karmic event in our life. There are a lot of other ways we can deal with this, but suppressing anger and closing our hearts to ourselves because we are angry is not one of them. We can trust ourselves when we acknowledge our anger, when we acknowledge our fear. When we open trust in ourselves, there's enough compassion and self-acceptance to work with these very powerful emotional pulls—they become our work on ourselves instead of a problem. These mind states are only a big thing when we feed them or fight them. When we cultivate the mindfulness that can accept them, we acknowledge our wholeness, and see it all as it is. Just more stuff, more bubbles passing through the vast space of mind.

There's nothing to hide from. We may say, "Gee, have I got that stuff in me?" But it's only "me" as long as we keep burying it. When brought into the light, it doesn't have power over us, it doesn't leap into action. When we have compassion and patience enough for ourselves to let such a state come up and be seen, it slowly disintegrates. Non-judging awareness has the power to see something as it is and let it go. When we can see it not so much as content, but as process, we recognize that all this emotional stuff we take so much to be us is really not so personal.

We don't have to be afraid to see anything. In a clear seeing of anger or fear or insecurity or doubt, each thing is defused, it doesn't beg for expression, its reactive power is dissipated. Mindfulness will cut through it. And the mindfulness weakens the force of its arising in the future, even though it may have such potency that it stays for a while. As we experience alternate moments of mindfulness and anger, we begin undermining the power of the anger.

Sometimes we become confused about how to respond to some persistent frustration. If, for instance, we're trying to make supper for our children and an uninvited guest has got his head in our refrigerator, mindlessly eating the food that was meant for the meal, we can trust ourselves to know what to do. We needn't put him out of our heart when we put him out of our house.

The nature of the mind is such that when awareness is present it displaces the kind of grasping that breeds frustration. We cannot have awareness and grasping active in the same moment. They don't fit in the same space. When we're not mindful, when we're identifying with the thought, which is forgetfulness, the opposite of mindfulness, we spin out. When we're mindful, each thought arises and passes away, to be followed by another—there's no stickiness. So, when we're mindful of anger, it won't stay. We don't suppress it, we don't act it out. We're just mindful of it, experience it, and watch it come and go.

Mindfulness is the most powerful agent we have for purification, because it cultivates non-grasping in the mind. It's interesting that in Buddhist thought they don't speak of cultivating lovingness so much as of developing non-hatred;

they don't speak of letting go so much as encouraging non-grasping. When those unwholesome qualities of hate and greed aren't in the mind, the natural state of loving-kindness and generosity is revealed. When there isn't hatred, the love that is always there in the wisdom mind becomes apparent.

Coming mindfully into the moment is accepting ourselves fully. We know that there are feelings we don't know the root of, feelings we're not in touch with: "I feel a certain way, but I don't know why; I have this uneasiness, but I don't know where it's coming from—and, here I am, just open to it, just sitting with it." We can allow ourselves to stay soft with that, not to close in on it, not to cause resistance in the mind and body. It's all right not to know—it leaves room for knowing.

We can experiment with our practice to see what's going on inside ourselves, for ourselves. We can observe what anger feels like, what joy feels like, what separation from the flow feels like, what fear or worry feels like. We can see what letting go does. We can experience all of ourself. We make room for all of ourself and return wholeheartedly into the flow with a self-accepting mind not caught in judging other mind states.

We allow ourselves to just watch the mind judging and see how judging, in the words of the Third Zen Patriarch, "sets heaven and hell infinitely apart." We see that the open space in which the contents of mind are occurring is of itself completely non-judgmental, non-opinionated, non-separate. It doesn't stop at this or that, it accepts it all. Judging breaks the original mindspace into a billion fractured pieces. By watching the judging mind with compassion, we mindfully cultivate self-acceptance.

10

The Hindrances

A hindrance is a blockage to the light of the wisdom mind. Rather than calling it "sin," it can be seen simply as an obstacle to understanding which attracts the attention, causing identification, and distracts us from an even-minded awareness of the flow. Hindrances are the basis for much compulsive reactivity, the seeds of much karma.

Though there are numerous hindrances, they are commonly divided into five major categories, five enemies, if you will, of the balanced mind. They are lust—which is a form of greed; hatred or anger—which is a form of aversion; sloth and torpor; agitation and worry; and—perhaps the greatest obstacle to investigation and clarity—doubt. Most of us have all these qualities to some degree, though often one is more predominant than the others. For instance, in the case of lust and hatred, greed and aversion, only one can be present at a time as they oppose each other in activity. If we're lusting after something, we're reaching for it, we're trying to devour it. If we have aversion for it, we try to push it away. Though the mind may change in a split second, we won't have both of these states in the same mind moment.

Greed is often a desire for pleasant states, for "more, sooner, quicker." It isn't necessarily sexual lust, although that certainly is one, easily recognizable aspect of it. It could even be lust after understanding, greed for certain subtle states of mind or peak experiences, or grasping after complimentary self images like "I'm a good meditator." The problem with this, as with all hindrances, is that it directs attention outward and therefore seldom recognizes itself. And, of course, without awareness of what's happening, it's very difficult for purification, for letting go, to occur. In a much subtler form we can recognize the quality of grasping as we drive down the road and notice that the eyes, without being directed to do so, are reading signs, are reading billboards, that there is a conditioned grasping of the mind at stimulation.

This is one of the predominant energies we notice in the mind—a grasping at objects, a thirst for experiences. Lust can be extremely painful to ourselves and often to the object we lust after if the object of our wanting happens to be another human being. Lusting either sexually, or, more subtly, for someone to serve as a reflection of who we think we are, causes that being to become an object of gratification, an object devoid of its wonderment, of its own intrinsic value. We are altogether separate from such objects of satisfaction, we feed from them, we use them. This is not to say that we cannot dance lightly with our desires, but the music must be heard by both and the hearts kept open.

The second hindrance is aversion or hatred, which includes fear. It's all we don't want; all the things we push away. When aversion is present, it stiffens the body and the mind. The aversions we feel, the prejudices we feel, the anger we feel, all push the world away. These aversions all resist what *is;* all block the free-flowing mind which knows things a moment at a time as they are and wishes nothing to be otherwise. Buddha likened anger—a most common form of aversion—to reaching into a fire to pick up a burning ember in our bare hands with the intention of throwing it at someone. Before the injury is done to another, it is done to ourselves. We notice when we watch anger that the object of anger is in some way wished injury, or humiliation. We really can't be angry at something or someone without wishing it harm. It's an unfortunate natural quality of this mental factor.

These hindrances, when seen clearly for what they are, don't create more karma. The sooner these states are noticed as they begin to take form in the mind, the sooner they can be let go of, the less power they will have to entice identification. If we know we are angry, without judgment, without aversion for that aversion, we can open the mind around it with the space that awareness offers and break identification with it. If we openly recognize and acknowledge aversion as it's occurring, we stop feeding the fire, and then it can only remain as the dwindling result of previous thoughts. Rather than being intensified, it burns out whatever old habits of mind caused it to be established in the first place.

When we watch the actions of these hindrances in the mind, we see they are not our friends. Though we may have a long-standing rapport with the hindrances, and think of them very much as ourselves—"my anger," "my greed"— they are just qualities of mind like any other. Seen in the light of understanding, they have less and less power to pull us into activity, to distract the mind. We can investigate these states of mind for ourselves. We can see how they take much magic out of the world.

Next we have our old comrades, sloth and torpor, which one teacher said was best personified by the banana slug. Sloth and torpor manifest in many ways. Usually, it's that dullness of mind that we experience now and again. Sometimes as we watch the mind we notice a great deal of drowsiness and dullness, which becomes quite an obstacle to clarity because without the proper energy, it's very difficult to penetrate. Sloth and torpor, like the other hindrances, can go so deep that it becomes a part of our character, a way in which we relate to the world. Sometimes it becomes evident to us when we're sitting and notice ourselves thinking, "Oh, that's plenty for now," or, "I think I'll stop; I've done enough." It's laziness. When it's present, it can block further work. It's a drowsy blindness which sinks into the mind in a very debilitating manner and often is identified with as "my tiredness" instead of being seen as "tiredness," as "torpor," and stayed with beyond the resistance which might arise in reaction to it.

Mindfulness is the most powerful means of cutting through any of the hindrances. We can sit with any of them, and, rather than blocking our meditation, they can become the object of investigation. It can be fascinating to watch tiredness or anger or greed if the mind remains soft and nonjudgmental. We can simply, gently, keenly observe this activity in the mind and body.

When mindfulness is not strong enough to cut through the hindrances, there are certain skillful means designated for working with them. With anger and aversion, the skillful means for neutralizing their intensity in mind is the letting go that occurs during the generation of feelings of loving-kindness. It is not uncommon for a teacher to suggest to a person who has much anger to establish a strong *metta* or loving-kindness meditation practice. In the case of greed, seeing the essentially unsatisfactory nature of grasping has the capacity to counter this quality in mind. For instance, traditionally those who had a predominance of lust were often directed to go to charnel grounds to observe decaying bodies and gain some insight into both impermanence and the object of their greatest desire. A less radical remedy, and one more suitable to our practice, is to encourage within ourselves moderation in food and sleep. This mindfulness of sensual gratification can often serve as an antidote to the yearnings of lust. When confronting sloth and torpor, taking a few deep breaths or even going for a walk may serve to reawaken a drowsy mind. Even just mindful standing for a bit may be of use. As a means of dealing with persistent torpor, a friend, while a monk in Thailand, was directed by his teacher to continue his meditation sitting on the edge of a deep well. Each time his head drooped, his eyes opened to see a gaping chasm before him. The torpor disintegrated very rapidly. Another friend walks slowly backward as a means of accomplishing the same survival alertness, as a means of overcoming tiredness in the course of long meditation retreats.

Restlessness, agitation, worry comprise the fourth hindrance. Agitation often comes in combination with worry about something. It's a considerable obstacle to clarity because the agitated mind has difficulty remaining concentrated. Most of us have experienced periods when the attention simply wouldn't stay with the breath, when the mind was off thinking about unpaid bills or recent arguments or what someone thinks about us or why we're restless. Again, as with the other hindrances, more self is created—more thoughts of "my worry," "my restlessness," "my boredom." This identification just creates more worry, agitated projections into the future, and a rehashing of the irretrievable past. The mind is lost elsewhere, out of touch with the present moment. The answer to very real problems can often be worked out, even thought through, more skillfully when the mind is allowed to quiet. Worry often blocks reception of the appropriate solution to the problem. Agitation can be seen very clearly as just another phenomenon of mind and let go of. The prescribed means of re-establishing the stillness of mind is the encouragement of concentration by gently returning again to the breath with patient perseverence.

Considerable patience is needed to work with these hindrances. They don't go away overnight. Baba Hari Dass says that even a ninety-one-year-old sage is not free from the hindrances. They come as they will, at any time. Much of our meditation is dealing with hindrances. To deal with them is simply to see them with a non-judgmental, open awareness.

Perhaps the most powerful of these hindrances is doubt, because doubt can stop practice. Though a little doubt can be useful to motivate deeper investigation of what we have been conditioned to believe is true, sometimes doubt can be so strong it closes the mind. We doubt that the method we have chosen is able to take us through. We doubt our own ability to understand. We doubt that freedom even exists. When doubt predominates, we stop working on ourselves. We sit back on our haunches and tend to feel sorry for ourselves and mistrust the universe.

Doubt can be so subtle we don't recognize it. We may indeed feel that meditation is all right for some people but our self-doubt somehow persuades us we just aren't capable of making progress. When we can see this moment of doubt as just another bubble of mind arising and passing away, it frees us from much of the confusion and tension in our lives.

I have a friend whose early life was very hard. Brought up in Spanish Harlem, she suffered much hardship and unhappiness. When she was eighteen years old, she found herself in India and somehow knew that she had to begin meditating to clear her mind. But she had such agitation and poor concentration, she could not sit for more than a few minutes at a time. Although most of the other hindrances were giving her a hard time, she had no doubt. Therefore she could do anything. She knew the work to be done and put herself to it. She had enough trust in the process to begin to let go of the content. It took her several months before she could sit a whole hour, but now she's one of the most extraordinary meditators I know. Her clarity and freshness of mind are admired by many.

The specific remedy, the skillful means, for doubt is often a little more understanding. Sometimes the reading of knowledgeable writings or talking to someone we respect will allay doubt or allow us to view the experience of doubt with a more spacious mind.

When awareness of the hindrances becomes keen, we know what's going on as it's occurring and the states of mind that used to overcome us become milestones of our growth. As the hindrances arise, they set off an automatic alarm in the mind which wakes us up and causes us to investigate the disturbance. They remind us how easily we get lost and how mindfulness keeps our lives simple and easy.

11

Giving

The greatest gift is the act of giving itself. Traditionally, three kinds of giving are spoken of. There is beggarly giving, which is when we give with only one hand, still holding onto what we give. In this kind of giving we give the least of what we have and afterward wonder whether we should have given at all.

Another kind of giving is called "friendly" giving, in which we give openhandedly. We take what we have and share it, because it seems appropriate. It's a clear giving.

Then there's the type of giving that's called "kingly" giving. That's when we give the best of what we have, even if none remains for ourself. We give the best we have instinctively, with graciousness. We think of ourselves only as temporary caretakers of whatever has been provided, as owning nothing. There is no giving; there is just the spaciousness which allows objects to remain in the flow.

We've all experienced these kinds of giving in our lives; giving from us and giving to us. We all know what it feels like when we hold on to what we give, when we're giving, attached to a particular response to the gift: "Will I be loved because I gave this gift?" We're attached to ourselves being the giver. It's not such wholesome giving.

We've also given when we felt it was just right to let something go into another's hands, just let it flow right through. That's the kind of giving that comes through people who are healers. They don't hold onto it—the life energy moves right through them. There's no one healing; there's just healing coming about. That's the kingly kind of giving.

More generally, as we grow into ourselves, we find ourselves giving, sharing openhandedly, and honestly. That feels good. That brings us to the kind of friendship, the kind of love that nurtures our growth.

Indeed, giving can become a whole practice in itself. It is possible to open ourselves to a kind of ongoing giving that holds nothing back, that allows us to give away even our anger and our fear. It is that kind of giving that we bring to practice, that we cultivate as we give our attention to the breath. That's the kind of giving that encourages spaciousness of mind. It is simply letting go, a non-holding which claims nothing for itself.

The most wonderful gift we can give is ourselves. To let go of ourselves so that we can experience what we are afresh each moment as though it were a gift. If we can treat everything that comes to us as a gift, as a kind of grace, then we can give ourselves away, holding to nothing, letting go lightly. We give the mind away, we give the body away. We just let it all disappear back into the flow as it passes by. We experience it all and give it all away.

Many times in our sitting, we become beggarly, we don't give ourselves away. We hold back, we resist certain states of mind, giving ourselves practice with the one hand, pull-

ing it back with the other. We're constantly checking
out how we're doing, measuring who we are now, evaluating.
But as we awaken, more and more we come to give ourselves
away.

And as we gradually give more of ourselves to ourselves,
we naturally give more of ourselves to others. There is a way
we are with people which makes it easy for them to be
themselves. We're not being someone who encourages
them to act in any other way. We're an open space, holding to nothing, giving it all away.

Buddha said that if people could really see the value of
giving, they would offer a part of every meal. The quality of
giving is so powerful that it loosens the stickiness of mind
and allows much light into murky corners. It creates an
openness of mind which encourages letting go and the
arising of wisdom. Making the mind as generous as possible makes it free and open and available.

As patience and the practice of giving slowly open us,
we are gradually able to give ourselves away, to let go of
anything which hinders our direct experience of the flow,
which blocks our understanding.

12

Watching from the Heart

It is quite difficult for the mind to uncover its own workings. The mind thinks, and we don't uncover the truth by thinking about what's happening. If thinking brought us to the truth, we would all be great sages by now because we've done all the thinking we can stand: we've thought about who we are and what we're doing and how to do it.

The stickiness and delusions of mind are seen most clearly when viewed from the heart. The heart does not label or manipulate, it just allows. It offers that patient, non-judgmental, non-clinging acceptance of each thought which allows the truth. When we note the contents of the mind from the warm spaciousness of the heart, we don't get caught by the mind's attempt to alter reality, to change its appearance with its constant commentary and rationalizations. The heart takes it all much more lightly and simply. When we try to beat the mind with the mind, it creates more of the same. The thinking mind turns the whole world into thought.

We're used to trying to control the world with our mind, to control ourselves with our mind. But we can't control ourselves with our mind and still be whole. Who has ever beat the mind with the mind? We just get afraid and angry inside; we've suppressed ourselves. We've suppressed *showing* that we're afraid or lonely, but that doesn't make loneliness go away. That just makes the pain remain hidden and not so accessible to our letting go.

If we're watching from the heart—from that openness—we're watching from a space of compassion that recognizes the mind as a natural process and does not even judge anger or jealousy or envy. It has less of a vested interest in who we appear to be to ourselves or to the world. It can hear what the lesson of the moment might be. The heart has room for everything.

Those who have some conflict between practices which seem to deal predominantly with the mind such as mindfulness meditation and practices which appear to work predominantly with the heart such as devotional meditation will find that when we deeply experience what's happening in the moment, we're aware of the workings of the whole universe. Then we see that "heart" and "mind" are convenient terms to use but can be limitations to our understanding if they become concepts which reinforce a fragmented mind. When the mind drops concepts it is not other than the heart. Then there is no heart and no mind; there is just our spacious, our natural, being.

13

A Gradual Awakening

An image useful to understand the process of awakening is of fruit on a tree. It ripens ever so slowly, day by day, until at last it's fully ripe and falls from the tree.

As we slowly awaken, we notice the maturing of certain qualities of mind. We may notice, for instance, the feeling of unworthiness, of distrust in ourselves, is diminishing, that we are experiencing a deeper level of being that is not so entangled in the daily melodrama. We notice that a lot of negative feelings such as fear and doubt that we have identified with for a long time have become a less prevalent force as the mind developed some larger awareness.

Upon entering into mindfulness meditation, a friend who had spent some years in devotional practice said to me, "I think my path has changed." The only reply that seemed suitable was that the path doesn't change; the path is always the heart, only the methods change.

My friend said he didn't want a method that offered only a gradual awakening, he wanted a great flash and to be done with it. This made me think of the story of the Zen monk who had for many years practiced very hard to attain enlightenment. He had worked and worked for enlightenment. One day, as he was digging in the monastery garden, his spade threw a pebble into the air which struck a piece of bamboo fencing around the garden: it made a hollow, clicking sound. Upon hearing that sound, his understanding of the nature of things was so profound that he became enlightened in that moment. Now, was that a sudden awakening, or was that the fruit of a gradual awakening? He had undoubtedly heard many stones hit many bamboo stalks before, but now he was ripe. It's the moments that have gone before that condition the degree to which we will be able to absorb the profundity of each moment which follows. Any moment could enlighten us if we would see its totality, its complexities, its simpleness. It seems to take a while before we clear the senses enough, clear our conditioning enough; to let go of models and perceptions so that we can simply hear, simply see, perceive deeply enough to understand the way things are.

So, the gradual awakening and the sudden awakening are not so different. Ramakrishna used an image of the freshly picked nut. When its husk is green, we could hit it with a stone and hardly dent it. But when that nut has ripened, just a tap and the shell will fall open. This is the gradual awakening that we're all participating in: ripening so that the shell can fall away and leave us free of our ignorance, free of our imagined self and its incessant posturing, open to the direct experience of the wisdom mind.

An analogy for this process of awakening and growth can be found in the classical Tibetan art form of the mandala. Though mandalas are intricate circular paintings, they can also be seen as representations of three-dimensional labyrinths. As we move toward the center of the mandala, we are rising as well. Because we usually think two-dimensionally, we think we're just going to jump to the center and that'll be the sudden awakening. We don't see the third-dimensional spaciousness, the gradual rising, the ripening that is happening everywhere at once.

Often, when we are confronted by some problem which arises again and again, we think we have somehow been fooling ourselves about any kind of awakening at all. "I still can't relate to my parents," or, "I can't wash the dishes without getting bugged," or, "I can't stop smoking," or whatever it is. We imagine we're still as asleep as we ever were. "Here I am, pulled just as hard, just as uptight, just as confused, without an answer." We don't recognize that what has grown is an awareness of our predicament.

Before, we were just lost in our problem; now, we're aware that we've got to work with it. That is awakening. When we don't know we're lost in it, there's no way out. When we're aware we're caught by it, we're already freeing ourselves. As we trust ourselves and experience this gradual awakening—not measuring it, or weighing it, or trying to taste it, but just seeing how it is without any score—it patiently steadies our feet on the path.

Practice is very much like a dance on a tightrope, balancing energies, awareness, concentration; balancing what is appropriate to the moment. In a moment of forgetfulness we fall from that tightrope only to find that we land on another tightrope. We fall from moment to moment. We discover that there's really just one moment, and that moment is now. In our awakening, we begin to experience the totality of that moment.

One of the last great Chinese meditation masters lived until he was 120 years old and died in the 1950s. In the course of his training he would spend ten years at a single aspect of the practice. He spent ten years circumambulating a mountain as one practice; he spent ten years working with a mantra as another practice. When he began to teach at the age of 70, he spoke of the patience of "the long-enduring mind." He said that we should practice as though we had ninety-nine more lifetimes in which to complete our work, but not waste a moment. In other words, we have our whole life to do the work, but we shouldn't let a moment of that life go by unnoticed.

When we start working on ourselves, there is a tendency to be judgmental of certain qualities of mind or perhaps to feel that we aren't accomplishing as much as we somehow imagined we might. In the beginning, there is much effort necessary to develop steady concentration, to become more aware, but there is another kind of trying which may slow down our progress because it creates expectation. Expectation is the opposite of patience. Expectation is waiting for something to happen; it is not a patient waiting. True patience manifests itself as a non-grasping openness to whatever comes next. It is a calm willingness to be present, to allow awakening to occur as it will.

As trying matures into patient resolution to devote energy to the practice without grasping at results, the universe slowly reveals itself.

14

Snaring Enlightenment

Sometimes we're so busy meditating we can't see the truth. We're so full of skillful means, ways of capturing the light, that we obstruct our natural wisdom with all our doing. Enlightenment is synonymous with the ability simply to be present, to be in the moment with no attachments anywhere else, with our whole life right here, right now.

We sit in meditation for an hour, but how much of that hour are we just sitting? How much are we thinking about how to sit, instead of just sitting? How much of the time are we lost in the thinking mind? To be able to just sit, to just be, is often very difficult. Most of our lives we've been encouraged to be elsewhere, in plans and strategies.

Perhaps all the skillful means and all the answers to all our questions just have to be gotten out of the way so we can get on with our work. Skillful means aren't going to get us clear as much as letting go of thinking that anyone or anything outside of us is going to do it, which comes from realizing that what we are looking for is already here. Even the wandering mind, if watched without desire for it to be otherwise, holds the key to great wisdom because it is exactly who we are right then. We needn't be anyone else.

When we experience the moment, we know truth, and that truth is applicable, is useful, in that moment. But we don't hold on to it because that truth is the truth of that moment. At another time, it might be an obstacle. So, too, methods are truths for a moment, tools to be used and then laid aside. Methods can be the means to cut through conditioning or they can become just an additional burden. Methods are like a thorn used to pick out another thorn. When the first thorn is removed from our flesh, both thorns are thrown away. All of the methods, all of the profound answers to all of the profound questions, are reflections of the moment to be seen and eventually let go of.

We can maintain commitment to a single practice without getting rigid or prejudiced. By trusting the inner sense of what is needed, we can maintain a deep relationship with the source we seek. Trusting the Buddha-nature, the heart of Christ, the essence of whatever lineage we follow, allows us even to be mistaken sometimes. Our addiction to always being "right" is a great block to the truth. It keeps us from the kind of openness that comes from confidence in our natural wisdom.

Zen master Suzuki Roshi spoke of the "enlightenment before enlightenment" which is the state of mind when mindfulness is present, when there isn't a grasping at things being any way at all except the way they are. It's just seeing the present moment, patient and straightforward.

When we employ some method to get us clear, we often dwell in the concept of an enlightened or unenlightened mind. We're still separated from our wholeness, we're still not in the moment. Enlightenment isn't enlightenment. Enlightenment is a word. One of the things that blocks us from whatever this enlightenment might be is our hunger for what we imagine en-light-enment to be. Enlightenment can become our greatest cause of suffering, because it's our greatest longing. It's our greatest "being elsewhere," our greatest vacuum. Enlightenment is freedom, the thought of enlightenment is prison. The truth exists in the moment. If we're anywhere else, seeking something outside of the moment, we're in prison.

I used to think that peak experiences were a sign of attainment. I'd have some new experience and sometime later have some other insight, and think, "Oh, it's really paying off, I'm getting closer now!" And then there'd be a floating experience and then an intense light experience . . . and each time the thought "Oh, here it comes!" And then there'd be the "unsurpassable wisdom world" and then the "no me at all, anywhere," and then another experience and another and I'd be saying, "Boy, it can't be far now!" And more and more experiences. Then I started to realize that I had thought there were going to be a few dozen experiences and that would be it, all finished, pure awareness twenty-four hours a day. But it turns out there are hundreds and hundreds of so-called "peak experiences." And they're all just experiences.

A friend whose meditation teacher had made quite a fuss over him in India because of several extraordinary experiences, returned to this country. Soon after he was back he went to visit a well-known Korean Zen master. The Zen master asked him how his practice was going. With some pride, he told of his many remarkable visions and in-

sights, and of the depth of certain moments in his meditation. The Korean master looked about the room, paused,
and asked, "And where are those experiences now?"

The value of depth experiences is the purification, the
penetration into what is, that occurs in the moment. But
clinging to any experience as an accomplishment or cap-
tured truth diverts the attention from the reality of the
next moment.

So how can we work toward enlightenment without the
clinging of desire? Unfortunately, in English we use the
word "desire" to mean two very different mental attitudes.
There's "desire" which craves enlightenment, perhaps seeking the satisfaction of an easier life, and there's "desire"
for all beings to be free from suffering, for the world to be
at peace. There can be the desire for purification which is
essentially a "motivation" toward completion. It's an open-
handedness, a willingness to receive rather than a desire to
be the first on our block to have cornered universal wisdom.
The desire for freedom, as it motivates us toward our natural
state, is great joy. The desire to be free from things as they
are is great suffering.

No one who wants to be enlightened will ever be enlightened because what we are enlightened *from* is that
someone wishing to be enlightened. Wishing to be enlightened is like the ego wanting to be present at its own funeral.
The imagined self, in attempting to possess enlightenment,
doesn't realize that it's committing suicide, for it is the
falling away of this separate "I" which allows the experience of our universal nature.

It's a gradual awakening, but, even knowing this, we
may at times notice our conditioning snap at a moment of
deep peace or clear insight, much like a fish jumping out

of the water to catch a bug. We can say to ourselves, don't reach for peak experiences because we know they're just part of the passing show, but nevertheless at times we notice the conditioned mind grasping to be something other than it is. But it's only this grasping, this constant becoming, that makes the mind seem unenlightened. When there's no grasping anywhere, that's it—that's the original mind, the essence of mind. Already pure. Already luminous. When we experience that for even a millisecond, it stops the world and allows us to let go of any need to be anywhere but in the perfection of the moment.

We all know more than we know we do. Wisdom is more accessible to us than we realize. We don't trust our vision because we think we are not enlightened. A friend of mine used to say, "Just go out and pretend you are enlightened. If you keep acting like you are . . . well, who knows?" Instead we pretend we are not enlightened.

But "not enlightened" and "enlightened" are both just thoughts. As we watch the mind, we see how shallow thought is because the movement of thought lies mostly in words. But at a deeper level there is a movement in mind which can be experienced when we are no longer relying on words, when we're just experiencing. At this level we experience an urge we could almost call a "homesickness for God," an ecstatic longing to come home, to return to the source, to be complete. This is the unconditioned endlessness beyond mind, pure undifferentiated being.

15

Mindstuff

The word "mind" is used in many different ways. Basically, it means the perceptual mechanism, but what we usually mean when we say "mind" is the thinking, rational, inner-dialogue mind, the "I am" mind, the ego mind. But that "mind" is only a part of a much greater intelligence that far exceeds what we call intellect.

The intuitive wisdom mind is that of a deeper level of being. Normally, we feel that we are only the thinking mind and give it undue attention, investing it with all of reality. But all of reality is not perceived at the thinking level of mind. We're always getting subtle input which we call intuition from the wisdom mind. We experience a deeper knowing. If the rational mind has no label for the subtler message, it has a tendency to discredit it. It disallows what it can't label. However, the rational mind can't label everything because it's not everything.

The insights that arise in the wisdom mind are often experienced as sudden, wordless understandings of how things are. This level of mind is not as dependent on the kind of "knowing" which traps reality in concepts and words. It can experience simply being. At times, walking alone in the woods, I have been only my moment-to-moment experience of being. As my foot touched the ground, the experience was all of reality. As my eye moved to a tree, there was only seeing—that was all of reality. A bird singing: just hearing. The fragrance of cedar: just smelling. It's difficult to describe the precision, the crystal clarity of it. Everything was silhouetted in the moment. Even the thought "Ah, look, everything's silhouetted in the moment" was another clarity silhouetted in the moment. Each thing was precisely as it was. It existed only in that moment of direct perception. It did not depend on the past for support or context—which doesn't mean it was without memory—it wasn't dependent on memory or thought of any kind to interpret the present. Nor was it leaning into the next moment. There was no desire for things to be any other way. It's very difficult to describe such experiences in words because they occur on levels where language does not exist.

As we gradually let go of our complete dependence on the rational mind, we let go of learning how to meditate and just meditate. Of course, the reasonable mind says, "Okay, I'll let go of the rational mind, but I need to know how. Please teach this level of mind to meditate so it can go beyond itself." So the mind absorbs the instructions and acts like a good servant: "Okay, I'll watch the breath to develop concentration."

"And, what do I do when my mind wanders?"

"Ah, I keep coming back to the breath, right?"

"Okay, got that."

"And, what happens when there's a pain in my leg?"

"Right."

"And, now what do I do when the energy is unbalanced?"

"Oh, that's a good idea!"

"By the way, what is enlightenment?"

"Oops, sorry, thanks."

On and on, learning. That's what the rational mind is good for: to collect and apply certain technical know-how—how to drive a car, follow a map, read a book, bandage a wound, learn to meditate. This level of mind is useful for learning and applying that learning to survival amid the complexities of the world. It is a good tool, a good servant. But, all too often, it becomes a terrible master.

As master, it becomes that which attempts to possess everything by labeling it, by thinking about it instead of directly experiencing it. This is the ego "I am" mind. It creates a separate universe with the conditioned after-thought which says, "I see, I taste, I touch." But it's just life that tastes, that touches, that is. The ego is a fiction, the outcome of the thinking mind trying to pull itself into the center as though it had a nucleus that was solid, stable, and unchanging. Where is the center of the mind? We seem to be limitless, a vastness with no boundary; therefore, no center.

There's no one place we can say, "This is me." Because "This is me" is just another passing thought. Though "I" is a convenient means of relating to inner change, where is there an "I" any other place? But the rational mind says, "Even though you can't find a solid separate self, there's one there." The rational mind is often irrational.

When some people begin to see the relative nature of the thinking mind, they say, "Kill the mind, the mind's my enemy." But that's the thinking mind speaking. Don't make "mind" the enemy. Mind *is* the meditation.

When we see thoughts coming and going, feelings

coming and going, sensations and memories coming and
going and going and watch them with a mind that doesn't try to possess anything, doesn't try to label everything, we are open
to understanding, and that is really all we have to do. Mind
will become focused in a very open way. It doesn't have to
be hard or stiff.

Mind doesn't have to be used to analyze where we are.
Just recognize it. Analyzation says, "Who am I now? What
made it that way? How did it get here?" Sometimes mind
will even attempt to trace its last thoughts to figure out
how it got to where it is. It's interesting, but it's just more
thinking. In fact, it's that interesting stuff that's kept us
going round and round on this merry-go-round for so
long.

There's an ancient Chinese curse that says, "May you be
born in an interesting time." If we're born in an interesting
time, our attention may be drawn out and we'll never get
down to the real work of uncovering our natural wisdom.
It's a curse to be lost outside of ourselves in mind forms.
We go round and round in this world, watching all the
melodramas out there, all the forms the mind projects but
seldom recognizes as the dream it is. Indeed, the whole
universe is mind. To be recognized as a form, it has to
arise in the process we call mind. Without this conditioned
thinking mind, things just are what they are, without commentary or evaluation, just pure "is-ness," with no label
to it, no "I" attached to "knowing" it.

But behind all these forms and dreams of the thinking
mind is a universal quality, an essence of mind which is altogether pure and without karmic accumulations. It is the
mind before thinking shatters it into a billion ideas and
preferences, a pure open space without attractions or aver-

sions. Perhaps its only quality could be described as "thusness," an openness in which all form originates.

It exists of itself, dependent on no conditions for its existence. It is pure essence—the direct experience of which leaves one with the understanding that awareness simply is. That we are not any of the contents of the mind. That beyond mind there is something other than anything the mind can conceive. That any thought of "I" or "body" or "mind," that any thought at all, is not who we are.

It is what some Zen traditions refer to as the One Mind, because it is shared by all beings. It is an unlimited reality, all of which exists within each of us. Quite beyond the relativities of space and time, it is the Original Mind: the mind before thinking, the mind before the universe takes form.

16

A Guided Meditation on Loving-kindness

(*To be fed slowly to oneself or read aloud to a friend.*)

Find a comfortable position in which you can sit for a while, one that isn't rigid or stiff, and just relax into your body.

Let your breath come and go of itself.

Now, reflect on the way anger makes you feel. Reflect on the fire in the body and in the mind which is anger. The separation that it causes, the isolation and the loneliness and the pain.

Anger comes from pain and goes back to pain.

Anger most often wants to do injury to its object, to the person or thing that it is directed toward.

Feel it in the body, in the mind; that turbulence, that suffering. The heart closed, armored against the world. Isolated.

Reflect on the painfulness, the separation which is anger, which is envy, which is jealousy.

Experience the tightness, the loneliness, the separateness of anger, the fire. Buddha likened anger to picking up a burning ember in your bare hands with the intention of throwing it at another, all the while being seared, burned by that anger.

Now, reflect on its opposite, on the qualities of warmth and patience which allow us space in which to exist, to flower. How the anger falls away, how the knots become untied, dissolved in that openness of warmth and patience.

With each breath, breathe in warmth, breathe out patience. Warmth being breathed in, patience slowly on the exhale. Warmth and patience. Warmth feeding you, nurturing you, allowing you to grow. Patience supplying all that room, all that spaciousness.

Feel the fire extinguished by this openness of heart. All the armoring gone. Warmth and spaciousness.

Now allow that warmth and patience to give rise to forgiveness. Reflect first on those who may have caused you pain in the past, either purposefully or by accident. Send them forgiveness. Easily now. Not by tensing or pushing. Allow those old curtains of resentment to fall.

Picture the person who somehow caused you pain, and say silently to yourself, "I forgive anyone in the past who, intentionally or unintentionally—by thought, speech, or deed—caused me pain." Forgive them as best you can.

If there's still resentment, accept that too; let it be dissipated as the light of forgiveness grows. Allow yourself to forgive. Let go of the pride that holds on to resentment. "I forgive you." Just let it go.

The power of forgiveness is so great. The power that has room to forgive.

Now for those to whom you may have caused pain. Ask their forgiveness. Not with guilt, but with understanding that we stumble, that we are all partially blind. Let go of your self-judgment.

And, silently to yourself as it feels right, say, "Anyone I have caused pain to, intentionally or unintentionally, through my thoughts, my speech, or my action, I ask their forgiveness."

Let all the rigidity that blocks the heart fall away.

Now, allow yourself to be forgiven. The stiffness in the chest, in the body, in the mind, is just resistance. Let it go. Let go of your resentment for yourself. Forgive yourself. Say "I forgive you" to yourself.

Make room for yourself in your heart. "I forgive myself for all the pain I've caused, for even the things I didn't mean to do."

Using your own name say "I forgive you" to yourself.

Gently, open your heart to yourself. Gently. Give it time. Self-giving. Bring forgiveness into your heart for yourself.

Make room for you. Envelop yourself in forgiveness and letting go.

Now, with that sense of openness, direct loving-kindness to yourself, in your heart repeat to yourself as is comfortable, with whatever words you find appropriate, "May I be happy. May I be free from suffering. May I be free from tension, fear, worry. May I be healed, may I be at peace.

"May I be done with suffering, done with tension, anger, and separation. Done with fear and hiding and doubt. May I be happy." Let you love you.

"May I be happy. May I let go of all the things that cause me suffering." Wish yourself well.

Say "I love you" deeply to yourself. Use your name if you need to. "I love you."

"May I be free from suffering. May I find my joy. May I be filled with love. May I come home to the light. May I be at peace."

Now, direct that love toward someone you visualize in your mind for whom you feel great love—a teacher, a friend, someone you like very much—picture them and reflect, "May you be happy. May you be free from suffering.

"Dear friend, may you be whole, may you come into your completeness. May you be free of anger, jealousy, tension, fear. May you be happy. May you be free from suffering.

"May you come into your joy, your fullness. May you be free from all suffering." Concentratedly direct well-being to that loved one.

Picture another being for whom you have love, whom you wish well. Picture them clearly, as distinctly and easily as possible, and direct your feelings of well-being to them, using some repetition. "Just as I wish to be happy, so might you be happy. May you be happy and free from suffering. May your tension, may your painfulness of heart, fall away. May your joy increase. May you be free from suffering."

Let that love expand to everyone in the house in which you are sitting. Fill the room with your love, with your care. Let the whole room, all these people, be in your heart. "May we all be happy." Don't forget yourself. You, too, another beautiful being.

Let your loving-kindness radiate out to everyone. "May we all be free from suffering. May we all be happy. May we each come into the light. May we let go of the blocks, may we let go of our suffering and experience our perfect being. May we all be free from suffering. May we all be happy. Free."

Let it expand outward. Let it include the neighborhood. Let it include all of the town you live in. Expansive. Spacious. Caring.

Let it keep expanding.

The whole country.

The whole continent.

Open your heart to it all. "May all beings be happy. May all beings be clear-minded. May their hearts open. May they be free from suffering." Slowly envelop the whole planet in your loving-kindness. Slowly and gently let your love spread to all beings, everywhere.

"May all sentient beings, all feeling beings, may they be free from suffering. May they love themselves. May they come to their happiness. May they uncover the joy of their true self. All beings everywhere.

"May all beings sit in the light. Free. Gone beyond suffering. May all beings heal into caring for each other. May all our wounds, all our suffering, be healed by the power of our love for ourselves, for each other. May we love each other."

Just let yourself sit in the light of this love, in this caring for yourself, for each other. Don't try to do anything. Just be. In love. In the light.

"May all beings share in this openness. May everyone experience this spaciousness, this openness of heart.

"I share the merit of this meditation with all sentient beings everywhere. May all beings know warmth and patience in their lives. May all beings know self-forgiveness.

May we learn just to be, a moment at a time. No expectations. Just an open heart. Sharing as we can.

"May all beings be happy. May all beings be free from suffering. May all beings be happy. May we all be free. May we all come home to our completeness."

17

Loving-kindness (Metta)

In the mindfulness meditation we're not encouraging the conceptual level of the mind; in fact, the conceptual level is simply watched. It's seen simply as the labeler. Loving-kindness meditation, however, does work with the conceptual level. In fact, it is perhaps the most profound usage of that level available to us. By filling that level with loving-kindness we purify it.

This meditation uses the conceptual, thinking, word-oriented mindspace as skillfully as it can be used. We cultivate a mental quality. We could cultivate any mental quality. We could cultivate envy, we could cultivate anger. Practice indeed makes perfect: practicing envy or anger intensifies the rearising of envy or anger; practicing love encourages the reoccurrence of loving thoughts in the mind.

In this case, loving-kindness is cultivated by recognizing the fiery characteristics of anger and by experiencing the openness, the quiet, of its opposite, warmth and patience. By recognizing areas of resentment and guilt, and letting go of our separation from others and our deepest self, we send first to ourselves and then to others feelings of well-be-

ing using such words as, "May I be happy; may I be free
from suffering." At first the words may seem pretty mechanical, just words. These words may also be met by our
feelings of unworthiness: "Oh, that's just self-indulgence,
that's a copout." When we first attempt to bring love to
ourselves, the idea that we don't deserve it is often quite
noticeable. The rational ego-mind may come up with various arguments to try to dissuade us from doing such a
meditation. These arguments arise from conditionings very
precious to watch. They alert us to much of what is blind-
ing us to the perfection, to the scintillation, of life. It's
this stuff that dulls us to our own beauty, that attempts to
convince us that we're really not worthy, that we're not
capable of enlightenment, that we're fractured beings who
are going to stay that way forever. There is a level in the
mind where such thoughts have been encouraged, have
been cultivated. Now we're cultivating something to replace them, and it's a much more powerful form of consciousness than the negative forms. It will displace them
with gentle perseverance and confidence.

In the beginning, such discouraged self-criticism and self-
denial are like hard-baked topsoil which is difficult to
penetrate but, once it is watered and turned and mixed
with a little nutrient, becomes the ground for great growth.
We learn to give ourselves warmth and patience and thus
to be able to cultivate warmth and patience. The nature of
these positive qualities is such that they will naturally displace less wholesome energies by themselves.

One of the ways of trying to cultivate loving-kindness
is by thinking of our own good qualities. I've worked with
people who have said, "I have no good qualities; there's
just nothing about me that's beautiful."

And I say, "That sure must be a drag, to feel like that, so unloved and unlovable."

"Yeah, it feels really awful not to be able to love anyone, even myself, even a little."

"There must be lots of people who feel like that."

"It's terrible for someone to feel like this. They're so lonely, so cut off from everyone."

And here's this incredible compassion for the human condition coming out of them. They are talking so lovingly about themselves because they have uncovered a care for the unloved which was always present but was previously inaccessible. Now they have recognized someone in need, and that someone happens to be themselves, and now they can direct feelings of well-being to that place within themselves which so wishes to be whole. And that's exactly how the meditation is done. We send love to this being who is so deprived of love and then radiate this loving energy out to all beings everywhere.

When I was first doing this practice and would find myself involved—becoming angry in an argument with someone—I would begin to send them loving-kindness, thinking that would cool them out, and thinking "What a good meditator I am." But I was angry; it was my suffering I had to confront. I was the one who needed the loving-kindness. So I learned that I had to generate love for myself first before I could open to another. To send loving-kindness to another I was angry at was an ego trip which just created more separation between us. I wasn't doing them any favor; in fact, my action had the subtle flavor of superiority and domination. But when I could make room in my heart for me, I could accept my anger or frustration without being threatened by it, and could allow it the space to pass away. This also gave the other person the space to let go of their anger. To send love to another we must first be in our heart.

The power of loving-kindness is so great that when we concentratedly send it out to another, they often can feel it if they are in a quiet place at that moment. It is a tangible but subtle energy which can be consciously directed, much like that quality of care which is the principal element in healing.

As practice continues to cultivate an openness of heart, we begin to experience the incredible power of this love. And we see that with all our imagined unworthiness and fear, with all our doubt and desire, it's hard to be loving all the time. But it's harder not to be loving.

18

Letting Go of Hell

Sometimes our sittings are heavenly, so clear and quiet. At other times they never seem to get still for very long. There seems to be a lot of motion in the mind and a lot of identification. We seem to get lost in the fire of mind. We tend to take that pretty seriously. We call it a good meditation or a bad meditation, perhaps not recognizing at the time the power of a "bad meditation," not recognizing the purification that goes on when the wandering mind or the agitated mind or the restless mind is uncovered. Just seeing it as it is gives us a lot of power over that state of mind. Power in the sense of an ability not to be caught in it, an ability to let go; having the power that counteracts the karmic push that made it come in the first place, a balancing power.

When people say, "Oh, I'm really getting there; my sitting is getting so beautiful, it's so wonderful, I can just sit all day," I think, "They're not experiencing all of themselves." It's really easy to get lost in those pleasant heavenly spaces, the pleasant states that come with deepening concentration, the tranquility, light, and peacefulness that come when the mind is steady. The mind is healing in those moments, and it feels very good.

But sometimes conditions don't offer as much energy for sustained concentration; distractions pull at the mind and don't allow concentration to be maintained or to balance with the energy, or awareness doesn't become constant enough to allow even-minded recognition. So, when I hear that every sitting isn't "super," I am relieved that the meditator has the opportunity to sit with the unpleasant stuff, a chance to watch the mind wishing it were elsewhere. Because that's the mind that creates the karma. That's the mind—the longing—that drives us from body to body, from incarnation to incarnation. That's the desire to be elsewhere, to have things otherwise.

When the mind is pleasant and pleasurable, we don't see that longing as much. We may not even notice our greed for enlightenment, our greed for higher states so clearly, our bondage, our slavery to a concept of being free, the suffering that's inherent in wanting things to be any other way than they are.

Our "bad trips," our hellish experiences, are often the most productive, most fruitful. When we sit and it's uncomfortable, or a fly is hopscotching on our forehead and we are agitated and the mind can't get balanced, though our practice has been deepening, it seems at that moment as though we've never meditated in our life. If we can then relax the body and just be there, we see purely the tension that pulls us away into the dark dream again, and we can let go. When you accept hell, it's not hell any more. Hell is resistance. Suffering is resistance to what is: non-acceptance.

We experience many forms of this hell as we watch the mind and body. And it is here we meet the demons of our impatience, of our greed, of our ignorance; the demons of our attachment to the idea that there's someone to get enlightened; the demons of our attachment to even knowledge and clarity which make it difficult after a good sitting or a good day to put up with the hustle and the noise and stress of a changeful life. The demons aren't the noise. They are our aversion to the noise. The demons aren't the impatience; they're our attachment, our aversion, our impatience with our impatience.

When you can accept discomfort, doing so allows a balance of mind. That surrender, that letting go of wanting anything to be other than it is right in the moment, is what frees us from hell. When we see resistance in the mind, stiffness in the mind, boredom, restlessness . . . that *is* the meditation. Often, we think, "I can't meditate, I'm restless," "I can't meditate, I'm bored," "I can't meditate, there's a fly on my nose." That is the meditation. Meditation isn't to disappear into the light. Meditation is to see *all* of what we are.

As long as there's any state of mind you prefer to any other state of mind, that's your hell. So, we sit and we say, "There's my restlessness," and we see it as the old demon. Not something to be afraid of, just the demon. The power of the practice is to cut through our attachment to that state. If restlessness is there, it needn't be our enemy. If we see restlessness as "I am restless," then it becomes a problem, then we've taken it on as a problem, we've made it our problem. Restlessness is just another part of our nature, our saying it's "our" restlessness.

One Zen master says, "If you think so, so; if you think not so, not so." If we think the demons are real and it's our stuff, then the demons are real and it's our stuff. If we think the demons are just puffs of smoke then we can effortlessly blow them away. But, too, if we think the Buddha is more real than anything else and become stuck in ideas of being or not being a Buddha, then even the Buddha becomes a demon, a blockage to the natural light.

When we see the flow is all there is, and become that flow—not being "someone" watching, but just being, nameless, just there with no identity—then there's neither demon nor Buddha, but just things as they are, perfect in their own way. We discover that as long as there is any part of ourself we're not accepting, we're not going to let go of hell and penetrate through all the phenomena that hypnotize us with pleasure and pain—all the thoughts of self, all the identification with body and perceptions and states of consciousness. Those aspects can't be seen clearly until we accept it all as it is, with a lot of self-acceptance and compassion. How many times have we been in the hell of "I'm glad nobody knows what I'm thinking." And yet, it's right in that moment that the opportunity arises for insight into how we manifest in the world, what keeps the inner world separate from the outer world, what creates heaven and hell. When you can just see thought, let go of thought, and come back softly to the breath, to the moment, gently and non-judgmentally—that's when the inner world and the outer world merge.

As we enter this flow and self-myths begin to disintegrate, to become less tangible, there may arise some terror. We imagine we are about to disappear into a void and wonder, "Well, what *is* happening then? What is real? I wanted to lose my ego, I wanted to lose my separation, I wanted my heart to open, but I am frightened now that there's no one here in control of things. What do I do now? Everything's out of control." But it isn't so much that the flow is out of control in the sense of being random as that it is out of the reach of some imagined "I" and is instead the perfect unfolding of the intricate laws of cause and effect, the law of karma.

By trying to control the uncontrollable, we create hell. And that's the fearfulness of the ego when it starts to fall away. The ego says, "No, I exist." But who we thought we were and how we thought we were doesn't exist in the way we thought it did, and it's scary. It's a new experience of just "is-ness." We see emotions come up and float through nothing, and we recall that that nothing is who we are. We experience a thought passing through this nothingness and wonder what's going on, but that wondering is noticed as just the next bubble floating through the open spaciousness we have for so long presumed was a solid, precious me. And we make a dash for something solid, and we grab back at doubt or fear; we create a demon to tell us we are real. The ego-self says, "I can't let go, I must be real; I mustn't be deceived." Doubt pushes away the flow, the wisdom and non-clinging, that dispels hell.

We imagine that things being out of control is hell, but when the openness and ease of the natural flow are experienced, all thoughts and feelings are equally consumed within the process and we are freed of the identification that creates "someone" to suffer. The hell becomes just another idea passing by with no more reality or substance than we give it credit for.

19

Pleasure/Pain and Happiness

There are various ways of skillfully dealing with pain which allow insight into how mind and body interpenetrate. When there is a pain in the body, we can see how it causes a state of mind. It encourages certain thoughts. The body affects the mind in the same way that the mind affects the body: just as our body posture reflects mood, so, too, body conditions create mental conditions.

When we look into pain the first thing evident is resistance to pain. We notice the physical sensation called pain and a mental response which is aversion to discomfort, repulsion. It's a desire to be in a state other than the state we're in, which is in itself perhaps the clearest definition we could have of mental suffering: wishing we were elsewhere. Wanting things to be otherwise is the very essence of suffering.

We almost never directly experience what pain is because our reaction to it is so immediate that most of what we call pain is actually our experience of resistance to that phenomenon. And the resistance is usually a good deal more painful than the original sensation. In the same way, we don't experience our tiredness, our boredom, our fear; we experience instead our resistance to them.

Our experience of these states of mind becomes coated with our conditioning. We never quite taste the things themselves because our conditioned resistance to them interposes itself and intensifies the aversion with yet greater distaste. Therefore, these states of mind are seldom incorporated into our wholeness and become constant interruptions in the flow. We often experience mind states that distract us from surrender, that abruptly put us back to sleep by causing an automatic aversion reaction. Dealing with pain in the body is an excellent way of starting to disengage that habitual reactivity to unpleasant states.

When we let go of that resistance—all the thoughts that come up, all the urges to escape—then we can just watch them, allowing them to arise in a spacious, soft mind. Keeping the mind soft so that it can cradle those thoughts of resistance allows all the area around the pain to soften as well.

If we've got a pain in the knee, we let it be soft all around the area of the pain. We direct attention toward relaxation all around the pain. The body pain creates a mind state that tenses, rejecting discomfort, then the aversion-tension reinforces tensing in the body. We get a ricochet effect, back and forth between the body and the mind, creating mental tension which causes physical tension, which in turn just intensifies the pain and continues tensing the mind. Tensing holds onto pain, which increases the pain while increasing the resistance to pain. There is pain and pain surrounding the pain.

But when we relax around the sensation, we relax around the associated thoughts. We let that pain be there. We recognize it and do almost exactly the opposite of what we normally do. Instead of evading the pain, we penetrate it. We go right into the area where the pain is with a concentrated, investigative mind. And, when we penetrate into the pain, letting resistance go, we see that pain is not a single monotonic laser beam of feeling, but, instead, an amorphous mass of moving sensations. It isn't just in one central knot, it's moving around the area and doesn't really stay in one single place. It is composed of multiple sensations.

As concentrated awareness enters the area and allows it to be as it is, we start seeing those multiple sensations as separate occurrences. We watch them moving about moment to moment, first one here, then one there. As the resistance leaves the mind, along with it goes the concept of "pain" and we can experience it simply as pure sensation. We can often penetrate into a place where it's just the arising and passing away of multiple sensations, perhaps experienced as just a tingling, the watching of which can be actually pleasurable.

Of course, all pains won't allow us that much spaciousness. Some pains will be so intense that they will keep capturing the mind. When this occurs, we watch the attention disappear once again into identification with the pain and observe the aversion of the conditioned response.

Our reaction to the pain in the knee, for instance, is symbolic of our reaction to most things which cause pain in our lives. We wish to escape them, to distract ourselves, to not deal with the unpleasant. And, thereby, we reinforce its power over the mind to distract us at yet another time.

When unpleasant states can't draw us out, we're on the road to freedom. And maybe that is because most of us have come to mistake pleasure for happiness. Usually we seek pleasure and avoid pain. But if we watch closely, we notice that pleasure doesn't make us happy. Pleasure is pleasure, a temporary gratification of desire. Happiness is a deeper satisfaction, a feeling of wholeness, of non-neediness.

The essence of pleasure-seeking is neediness, a longing for satisfaction, a feeling of living in a vacuum always moving toward pleasure-giving objects, always grasping at straws. The seeking of pleasure is probably our greatest cause of suffering. When we closely observe mind, we notice that if there is an object we want, inherent in our wanting and not having it is a feeling of dissatisfaction, a tightness, a discomfiture.

It is interesting to notice that even in the satisfaction of desire, gratification occurs only in the process of moving from not-having to having. Upon having, there's no longer satisfaction. The process of satisfying the wanting occurs not in the possession of the wanted object, but in the cessation of the painfulness of desire. In the possession of that thing, there is no inherent satisfaction. Much of our experience of pleasure is overcoming the discomfort of desire. When the wanting has ceased and the object is at hand, there then arises the pain of wanting to keep it, wanting nothing to mar it, to break it.

Moving from not-having to having is the predominant experience of satisfaction our desire system affords. It's in the change, not in the object, that satisfaction occurs. But seeking pleasure is not seeking happiness. We're seeking happiness in the uncovering of mind, of desire itself. At times it may not even be pleasant to meditate, but it nurtures our happiness by uncovering our essential nature, allowing us to reside in that completeness. It is that spaciousness of non-wanting that is happiness.

However, it's important to recognize that even in what we call spiritual paths there exists the same elements that distract us in our wordly life—our addiction and attraction to pleasant experiences and our repulsion and aversion to unpleasant ones. Watching peaceful states is a lot more agreeable than watching our greed or selfishness. In fact, one of the reasons that concentration is so pleasurable is because the craving of the hindrances is suppressed by the stillness. Quiet is often too seductive for the restless mind. The power, the strength of mind that concentration creates, doesn't allow the hindrances much activity.

Attachment to this quietness can become a problem. So seldom at rest, the mind grasps at the deep pleasure of this stillness. Quiet is often too seductive for the restless mind. to want to go on with its work. It's wonderful just to turn on the lights and go out of the body, go out of all the pain in the body and in the mind, and just hang out in the bliss or stillness. But attachment to these states is a subtle form of discontent. If nothing is moving in the mind, the opportunity for understanding what binds us does not occur.

There is a practice called "sitting through pain," but I don't think that's what we need to do. That particular practice has the danger of creating a lot of self. "I sat through pain." If it's an endurance test, you just create someone to endure, and increase resistance and pain. Yet, it sometimes seems that the painful stuff can wake us up more readily than all the light and bliss. It's easy to go to sleep in the pleasure, but it's not easy to go to sleep in the pain of a sore knee or our hatred or our greed or ignorance. When we learn to skillfully use our pain, without creating an endurance test, we see our difficulties very clearly; they wake us and remind us how easily we get lost in our conditioning.

So we learn not to hold on to even our pain. Oddly, it's often easier for us to give up our pleasure than our pain. It's easier to give up our sex life, our hot fudge sundaes, or the pats on the back and such, than to let go of our pain, fear, and insecurity. We identify with them, we really hold on to those conditionings.

The American Indians made a rather small, round structure to use as a special sweat lodge. The participants crowded close together inside with their backs bent to suit the low roof. Often they were down on their knees, hunched over in this unbearably hot steam. Yet, they had vowed not to leave, so the only alternative to going crazy was just to let go. They didn't dwell on the impossibility of standing any more. If they had, they wouldn't have made it. Instead, they overcame their resistance by going directly into the experience of the moment, entering pure sensation. They used discomfort and their resistance to it as a method of pushing past their limitations, but they did it in such a way as not to create more ego. It forced them to go beyond whatever and whoever they imagined themselves to be, to become totally open to an experience beyond themselves.

When we let go of the resistance, we penetrate to the direct experience of the distraction, and its quality of distractedness, its discomfort, dissolves in the clear seeing of it.

When we go beyond the attachment to pleasure and

pain, allowing the long-conditioned responses to be met by awareness instead of being compulsively acted out, we experience a deeper happiness. An opening of the heart and mind occurs, a feeling of fulfillment in the moment.

20

Karma

Buddha said that the root of all karma was volition, motivation, the intention behind an act. What we popularly call karma is the result of what has gone before. It is the effect of a previous cause, quite mechanical and impersonal in its occurrence. "This arises, that becomes" was how Buddha defined karma.

"What's my karma? Is it my karma that I am healthy? that I am rich? that I am sick? that I am deformed? that I am crazy? that I am not crazy? that I am successful?" We have a lot of questions about what our karma is, misunderstanding perhaps that karma is not something outside ourselves. It's not luck or coincidence, it's the perfect outcome of previous input.

We don't have to go to an astrologer or a palmist to discover what our karma is. Our thoughts are our karma. Our likes and dislikes are easily seen as our karma. There are a hundred likes and dislikes, a thousand opinions, ten thousand concepts about how things are that have been conditioned by previous experience. All these likes and dislikes drive us from action to action, creating more karma, more causes for future results.

There is little you can do about what arises in the mind. What arises is karmically conditioned by what has gone before. There is nothing that need be done about any object as it arises. There is only something we can do about how we respond to that object. How we respond creates the next moment, and conditions how that same object will be related to in the future.

The sooner we notice the arising of moods and thoughts and realize they are just karmic fruits of the past, the easier they can be let go. There's no need to reinforce these states by reaction, to become as Trungpa Rinpoche says, "negative in the negative." When negative, unwholesome states arise, don't hit at them with a hammer. Don't get angry at yourself for being angry which only creates more karma. We can learn to respond in a skillful manner that allows compassionate recognition of our conditioning to pull us out again and again. Then we can begin to understand why we will find ourselves angry, jealous, selfish, greedy so many more times. And how many more times we are going to find ourselves without such unwholesome tendencies, and think, "Ah, I'm done with them at last." And how that greed for being "done with them at last" will create the next state of mind. How letting go of it all is really the only way.

In the course of life certain things are karmically given, one of which is that with every object of mind there arises karmically conditioned feelings of attraction or repulsion or, at times, indifference. We usually either like or dislike our experience. With every sense impression, with each thought, there is a subtle leaning toward or away from each object in the mind which is karmically determined.

Because we're in a body we have senses; because we have

senses, there is sense contact; because of this contact there is perception; because of this perception there's recognition, which then conditions the arising of feeling, of liking and disliking and the subtle emotional response to what has been perceived. These are all unavoidable karmic givens. But out of this liking and disliking comes craving, which forges the grasping that conditions the next link in the karmic chain. If your conditioning is that you don't like it, the desire will arise to push it away, while if you do like it, the desire will occur to pull it toward you. Desire conditions the arising of the urge to do something about it—the volition that leads to action. It is the clear recognition of that feeling of liking and disliking, without reaction, that cuts the karmic chain.

As we recognize the mind's automatic interest in the objects within it, a clear awareness of the process can decondition the mechanical continuation that leads to more karma-creating activity. Liking and disliking is the result of previous liking and disliking, the resultant fruit of past preferences, and leads to more of the same. It keeps the karmic wheel turning, creating more activity by conditioning more desire and craving. But when awareness penetrates the arising of feeling, of attraction and repulsion to phenomena, the karmic pull into more action is weakened at that very point where wanting conditions the volition that energizes activity. Deeply seeing this level of being recognizes the fruit of past karma as it is without any need to take it further, any need to compulsively act on it and continue its arising.

So we see that likes and dislikes are karmic, that we like some things and we don't like others. We like what pleases us; we don't like what displeases us. Gradually we get so that we can watch liking and disliking with clarity. This clear seeing may be experienced as pleasant although the object noticed is unpleasant. The greater the degree of awareness, the less the degree of grasping. It's psychological physics. When awareness is strong, grasping isn't. And when grasping is weakened, volition toward unwholesome actions has little intensity.

Because karma is based on volition, on intention, it is easy to see that if our intention is to harm others, we will be wary of being harmed ourselves. We will incur paranoid thoughts. It doesn't necessarily mean that somebody is going to trip us as we walk around the corner. We trip ourselves. We don't have to go anywhere to look for our karma. We are our karma.

The awareness just to notice intention is quite subtle. As we've said, normally we scratch without knowing we itch. But eventually, if we notice the intention to scratch, we will recognize before it the itch. The advantage of recognizing the itch is we then have choice—the choice of scratching or not scratching. Now, if it isn't an itch, but an action which is harmful to someone else or to ourselves, we have the choice to act on it or not act on it. Being aware of that level of mind changes our relationship to our conditioning, our karma. It allows us more space in which to respond.

Awareness of even unwholesome action brings us closer to not repeating it in the future. If we are not telling the truth, for instance, and at least know we're lying, we're closer to uncovering the cause for it. If we're lying and don't know it, we aren't even near understanding the root motivation for it. We're that much further away from un-tying that karmic knot. Developing awareness means not only knowing that we're involved in a certain action, but also recognizing the intention which that action is a response to.

But such motivations are not something to ponder. We either see it in the moment or we don't. It's not the analytical mind or 20/20 hindsight that uncovers the karmic root of the moment. We just watch our mind, and if we see it, we see it. And if it's not apparent, we just notice what follows. If it's important that we unlock a specific motivation, that we clear some persistent patterning that has caused us grief, we may then employ contemplative investigation. It's best not to get lost in a "Why did I do that?" round of thinking, because that's not being present to the process of the moment in which the karma is unfolding. Then we recognize wondering as just a moment of agitation in the mind.

The act of giving is a good example of not losing our way in motivational analysis. I'll find myself in acts where I'm giving and I'm very aware that I'm giving, and realize it's not being done in the greatest purity. I recognize a certain self-consciousness that I'm the giver: "Ah, this is a 'good' thing I'm doing." But I realize that if I waited until I could give with only the greatest purity, the clearest non-attachment, I probably would never get out of my chair. Accept that there are going to be motivations that are not altogether selfless, but yet may aid in the development of that openness. Don't judge intentions; simply recognize the energy behind the activity. We often have the choice to act or not act if we're seeing intention, though some-

times the karmic pull is so great that we notice it and still get
lost into doing it again. But that's okay. The deeper the
awareness, the deeper the purification. The deeper the
awareness, the more natural the ability to let go, the greater
the open-handedness.

We're in a society that is so psychology-ridden that it's
almost hobbled with "Why did I do this and that and this
and that?" Although psychology has a powerful cleansing
function, like any method it can become a trap, and it's
trapped many of us in the West. But the more we act
from the heart, from that deep intuitional space, the less
the spinning of the mind will interfere. The more awareness with which we do something, the more heart we act
on, the more that self-acceptance will allow us to trust
those acts.

When I was teaching in Soledad prison, there were many
questions about what karma was. The inmates often asked
if it was their "karma" to be in prison or why they were in
prison for a minor offense when they'd done things much
worse. Why didn't they get caught for one of the big ones?
A few who were innocent of the crimes they were con-
victed for asked had they done something "bad" in a
previous life. What caused the first karmic act which led
to all the rest? The Buddha said the question "What is
the beginning of karma?" is imponderable, the investigation of which would unhinge the mind. Certain things
happen to us as a natural response to things that we've
done before. And sometimes the things that we've done
are untraceable. It helps to not get lost in an analytic
labyrinth or get caught in an ache to know what does not
seem knowable. Dealing with the resultant fruits as they

ripen in the present moment by using an adequate and appropriate response to what's in the mind allows us to trust ourselves enough to know what to do.

It may sometimes be pleasant and other times painful, but it's actually perfect. At times when concentration and awareness are deeply balanced, the perfection of this karmic process can be experienced and it can be clearly seen that things could not be otherwise though often they may appear meaningless. We can learn to trust the perfection of the unfolding, even though sometimes it seems so hard.

"How am I going to untie this one?" We have some karmic knots that are so intense that every time they come up, we react. Then, at other times, the pull is less and we think, "Oh, I'm over it," only to find the pull twice as strong next time. But things are unfolding just as they must and, though they may sometimes be difficult, they are always the perfect opportunity for work on ourselves at that moment.

When some Buddhist teachers speak of "non-action," they are not recommending that we find a hammock on a deserted island. Non-action does not mean non-doing. Non-action is the disengaging of self-oriented volition from the karmic chain of activity. Non-action means acting without a sense of "self": appropriate but not attached action. Non-action is doing what's right in the moment. Action is the grasping of desire at some satisfaction, the intention for some result that will satisfy craving. Non-action is just being with what's happening in a non-interfering manner.

If our way in the world is led by compulsive, self-oriented action, a blind protectiveness is generated by our reactive attitude. If our way tends toward harmonious non-action, a spacious peacefulness is generated by our non-grasping attitude. Our actions will be mindful actions which create more awareness.

> All that we are is the result of what we have thought: it is founded on our thoughts, it is made up of our thoughts. If a man thinks or acts with a selfless thought, joy follows him, as a shadow that never leaves him.
>
> —Buddha, as recorded
> in the *Dhammapada.*

21

A Sense of the Absurd

Sometimes we take our sittings so seriously. We think in terms of "my progress," shortsighted to the gathering power of awareness and the universe in which progress is happening. We lose sight of the joy of our growth. But the expansiveness which comes with understanding creates a lightness that sees beyond all our self-centered attempts to overcome the imagined self.

When we're "working hard on ourselves," we sometimes push away our easy mind, our happiness at being on the path in the first place. We lose the sense of our absurdity which can serve as a balance to the seriousness of our practice. When we lose that openness to the cosmic humor of it all, we lose perspective. We become like the rooster who thinks his crowing makes the sun come up each morning. We think it is "me" beating "the ego" rather than appreciating the universe coming home to itself. The whole melodrama of our attempts at capturing freedom benefits greatly by the balance a well-developed sense of the absurd allows the mind. Indeed it is said that the angels can fly 'cause they take themselves lightly. A bit of aerodynamics it is well for all of us to remember.

The sense of humor that develops with a deeper perspective of our predicament is often a key element in the ability to let go. Don Juan talks about "controlled folly," which is his way of expressing that sense of the absurd which honors the miracle of even being here to do work together.

That's a very balanced recognition. We do what we do, knowing it's going to turn out as it does quite beyond our control, not grasping at any result other than the act's natural outcome. To be able to dance when dancing is called for, to be able to sit when it's time to sit.

It's the cosmic farce, that unknown newness which keeps us right on the edge of our seats. It's the deep, caring laughter of a non-interfering awareness, which watches us trying to figure out the cosmos with the rational mind, which is something like the tail trying to wag the dog. Staying light in the face of truths that appear to contradict each other, maintains respect for the natural unfolding of things, without trying to control the flow.

We maintain our practice, our investigation of what seems real, even when we come face to face with the seeming contradiction of its paradoxes, and know all we can do is take one breath at a time and watch what comes next. Our experience of exerting considerable effort in order to enter an effortless consciousness or having to choose to develop choiceless awareness leaves us feeling a bit perplexed by it all. Floating just beyond the boundaries of what we might at times imagine to be altogether sane, the thought "Is this all making me a little schizoid!?" passes through a mind that is not identifying with its contents but just notes "thinking, thinking"—"Hey, what's real!?"—"thinking, thinking"—every thought of who we are, unable to be accepted, to be held onto for more than a millisecond—yet here we are, and the rational mind doesn't know which way to turn and the heart couldn't care less. The perfect absurdity of it signals that somehow we're on the right track. And our status in the world becomes somewhat like that of the Sufi teaching figure. Nasrudin, who goes into the bank to cash a check. The teller glances at the check and asks, "Can you identify yourself?" Nasrudin pulls a small mirror out of his coat pocket, holds it up, and, looking into it, says, "Yup, that's me all right."

22

A Guided Meditation on Energy in the Body

(To be fed slowly to oneself or read aloud to a friend.)

Bring the attention to the top of the head. Feel the sensations arising of themselves at that place which is soft when we are born.

Feel that life energy at the crown of the head.

Feel the physical sensations arising. Not grasping, just allowing awareness to uncover what is already there. Feel the soft tissue of the brain held within this bony case. Brain stuff. Matter, full of sensation. Full of the life energy.

Feel the layers of skin that cover the skull case. The flesh of the cheeks and the skin on the brow. The chin, the lips. Matter, full of sensation. Feel the whole head. Feel its hardness, its solidity. The whole head, supported on the neck.

Direct the attention to the muscles of the neck. Not the thought of "neck," but the feeling arising there. The energy generated. Feel neck. Windpipe. Feel the breath passing through the windpipe generating sensation. Watch life in the neck, in the windpipe.

Experience the shoulders. The flat bones of the shoulders, as they round to form the large sockets for the armbones, covered by muscle and skin; generating warmth, solidness, vibration in the body.

Feel the chest and ribs.

The belly.

The whole back, the spine and the shoulder blades. Feel the sensations generated moment to moment by life in the whole torso, in the body. Feel its vibration, its scintillation.

Feel the intestines inside the body cavity. The stomach. The bladder. Feel the soft matter inside the body case.

Perceive body as vibration, as heat and solidness.

The arms: just sensation. No idea or designation "arms"; just the feeling, just sensations received from life in the body, from the shoulders to the hands. Feel the activity concentrated in the palms, in the fingers—vibrating, pulsating. Pure energy inhabiting pure form.

Feel the pull of gravity on this body form. The heaviness of the buttocks on the pillow, the sensation of solidness at the point of contact with the floor.

Open to the sensations arising in the legs, the legbones nestled into the leg sockets, the legs to the ankles. The muscle, the flesh, the bone. Full of sensation. Charged with sensation, with life. The tops of the feet and the soles of the feet. Sensitive and alive. Full of feeling.

Now, bring the whole body within the field of concentrated awareness. Allow sensation to arise as it does anywhere in the body: in the head or shoulders, in the arm or torso, in the hips, the pull of gravity against the pillow or against the floor, the legs, the feet, the hands.

Experience the energy shared by us all. Experience the

common flow of life vibrating in the body, animating the body.

Experience the pool of life energy in this room.

Open to your experience of it, however it's happening. Enter the vast space of energy within the body. Let go into it. Let go into the life energy. Let your body go into the life flow itself.

If the sensation of the life force changes, change with it. No resistance, no separation. Pure sensation, pure form. No body. No mind. Let it all go into the vast space of the life force.

Don't hold onto anything. Not hearing or tasting or smelling.

Let whatever is keeping you separate—a thought, feeling, expectation, desire, judgment, fear, anger, doubt—go back. Don't claim it. Don't hold onto it. Don't be afraid. Let go into it. Let go into the flow itself, into us all.

Don't hold onto a single thought. It all belongs to the energy of life, of awareness in form. Let it go back. Don't hold onto these words. Let them all go back into the flow of the life force. The common flow. Just life. Let it all come; let it all go. Don't hold on anywhere.

Subtler and subtler, just let it be. Let go into it. Disappear into it. Don't hold on. Just go into it. Surrender your separateness. Merge into the wholeness of it.

Let go of the mind; let go of the body. The breath just coming and going, expanding into nowhere, returning nowhere; just moment-to-moment being.

Mind comes and goes. Bubbles pass through. Nothing sticks. Nothing stays even for a millisecond. Let it all go. Merge back into the single force, into the one mind, the one body, the energy of awareness itself.

Experience everything as it arises and passes away, simple and easy, coming from nowhere and going nowhere. Just the flowing through vast space. Completely full; totally empty. Vast and immeasurable, simply being.

There is no separation anywhere but in mind.

We exist everywhere at once, perfect as is, complete.

23

Opening the Body

The environment we live in most is the environment of which we're least aware: the body. When our attention is placed at different points in the body, multiple sensations are perceived, sensations that are always occurring but are usually just below the level of conscious awareness. The attention isn't causing those sensations, it's merely uncovering what's already there. The incessant chatter of the mind and the constant externalization through the senses distract our recognition of the reality of the body.

But, as we become aware of what's going on in our lives and in the world about us, we also come to perceive what's going on in our bodies and we find that our bodies are not so different from the rest of the universe. We can discover the universal laws within our bodies as well as our minds.

As perception becomes very subtle through the intensification of concentration and directed awareness, we discover for ourselves one of the four "basic realities" which Buddha delineated.

The first of these realities is the elements of which we are composed. We experience the earth element, our solidness: the heaviness, the thickness of our substance.

That's the feeling of the buttocks heavy on the pillow or the bench. It's the feeling of the pull of gravity on our body, the heaviness of the arms or the stiffness in our neck. It's something that is real, that we can experience. It's not an idea or concept, but a direct experience, therefore it can be considered a basic reality.

We experience the air element as vibrancy, as energy. We feel the pulsation, the scintillation of the body, as the cellular structure is constantly being born, existing, and passing away. We can feel universes within us coming into existence and passing away, just as we can discover them in the sky. We can feel cells being fed and dying and being replaced. It's all experiential.

The water element is the cohesive element. Its binding quality is subtle though and less easily directly experienced. Its action is likened to that of dry flour that won't stick together; when water is added, then the cohesive element becomes present. It allows the mass to hold form, shape. It is the blood and lymph and cellular fluids of the body.

The fourth is the fire element, and it's experienced as heat or cold. It's what produces temperature and allows us to use nutrients in the body.

All four elements compose all matter, and are present at all times, although one most often predominates over the others. We notice ourselves being hot or warm or cold, but still there's the feeling of substance, of solidity. There's still kinesthetic input coming in from the earth matter. We still feel the vibration of the air element in the body.

The second of these four basic realities is consciousness, the knowing faculty which meets each object of the senses as it occurs, and can be perceived constantly rising anew in the ever changing flow of mental impressions.

The third is the group of mental factors, the qualities of mind such as anger, love, hate, concentration, mindfulness, doubt, joy, shame, restlessness, faith, energy, etc., that determine how consciousness relates to its object.

It is the interplay of these physical and mental realities that comprises our experience of the world. Our experience of the first three realities, all of which are conditioned by the ways we've experienced them in the past, opens the way to the experience of the fourth.

The fourth reality is not conditioned by anything that has gone before. It is an unconditioned state, called by some nirvana. Whatever name is used for this state, the name is not the reality. The name is still in form, the condition is formless and cannot be held in language. Even words such as "eternal" or "infinite" denote time and space, concepts which are not relevant to this reality.

But, of course, there is only one reality, only one truth, and that is the present moment. If we are living in our body, aware of what's occurring in the field of sensation, then we're in touch with the basic reality of existence as it is received in the present.

When awareness is open in the body, we tend not to get so lost in our head, we don't get so confused by the flux of mental conditions and states of mind. Staying at the level of sensation in the body allows us to see everything much more clearly within that field of awareness. It's the perfect backdrop. It's a non-verbal level of awareness which is available all the time.

Actually, the sensations in the body can be used in the same way a mantra is used. We can live in these sensations to such an extent that we're always aware of our body, of the life force that animates us. And anything that interrupts this awareness is clearly seen as a separate phenomenon.

Eventually we see that mind and body aren't so separate, aren't so different. The field of sensations in the body can be used like a Wilson cloud chamber, which contains a fine mist in which even the subtlest cosmic particle can be tracked. We can't even see the particle, but we can recognize it by the trail it leaves. Likewise, we can feel thoughts in the body. We begin experiencing thought and mental states throughout our whole system; then, feeling and thinking become aspects of the same process, not so different from each other. Unfortunately, many of us are so dulled to our body that we hardly ever experience this level of awareness unless we experience the grossest sort of emotion, like fear or anger.

The body holds the mind just as the mind contains the body. Deep feelings of loss and pain are recorded in the tissues of the body as well as in the mind. In deep quietude, the mind can free the body of its holding, just as in deep grounding and surrender the body can unlock the deepest secrets of the mind.

The body can become a very sensitive diagnostic tool. It can signal what's happening to us. It can even detect the experience of others as we pick up, on the feeling level, the mental states of those around us.

To cultivate this awareness, bring attention to the level of sensation and, throughout the day, note the sensations that are received while maintaining some recognition of body postures. Simply knowing what posture we're in, noticing when we shift our weight to stand, knowing when we're standing or sitting, knowing where our hands are, being aware of the position of our head, aware whether our eyes are open or closed, has a very powerful awakening quality that brings our experience directly into present reality. It sounds so simple, but we're probably not conscious of our body reality even a dozen times a day.

As we come more fully into the body, into an awareness of what is being felt, we awaken enough to our inner response to conditions to recognize what's needed. We check back to this finely tuned diagnostic mechanism to see what is called for, how balance can best be maintained. We learn to read ourselves by feeling and listening deeply to how we are responding to what's coming our way. We follow the subtle messages received, feeling when we are out of harmony or heading in that direction. A good example of this is that feeling we notice as a conversation turns from friendly talk to slander or derision of another: the stomach tightens slightly, the chest stiffens. It doesn't feel right, something is obviously out of tune.

We can be guided to a clearer way of acting in the world, toward more honesty and straightforwardness, by noticing how the body subtly responds—how it isolates or opens, how it tenses or relaxes during certain activities. Through this attunement, a deep abiding virtue develops naturally, an inner sense of what is appropriate and necessary to maintain harmony at any given moment. It is a morality quite beyond precepts and commandments, a natural way of action, a harmonious participation in the present.

24

Daily Practice

A daily meditation practice seems to be a necessity for the development of awareness and clarity. Sitting for thirty minutes or an hour in the morning after we arise, before a lot of words have come through us, is a perfect way to begin the day. Indeed it's interesting to notice when we sit first thing in the morning that even though we've had a whole night's sleep, levels and levels of relaxation continue to occur as subtle tensions are released. It becomes obvious that the mind is working and the body is affected, even at our time of greatest rest.

It is common for people who have recognized the value of developing a daily meditation practice to sit both first thing in the morning and again before going to sleep at night. As practice develops, we would not leave the house in the morning without sitting any more than we would without brushing our teeth, and out of the same self-respect. The evening sitting allows a clearing of the day's accumulations and a deeper penetration into the ways in which the world affects our being.

As we attempt to establish a daily practice, it may sometimes be difficult to sit. We see the thought, "I'm too restless to sit," but we allow ourselves not to act on the mind's intention to get up and distract itself. It's useful to sit and watch the mind seek satisfaction and attempt to elude the unpleasant. So we sit and watch restlessness. Restlessness becomes the meditation. Actually it can be a phenomenally interesting meditation to watch restlessness because restlessness and boredom are different aspects of the same agitation in mind which repeatedly wishes to get up and *do* something, to fulfill its desire. But when restlessness and boredom can't force us to act, when we have allowed change to replace even these discomforts, then the chain of blind desire into blind action begins to disintegrate. We no longer find ourselves thinking, "Why did I say that? Why didn't I trust myself? How could I let myself fall into that one *again?*"

In the attempt to understand the nature of such deep drives, we can set aside some time each day to meditate, to investigate ourselves. I know many people who sit only a few times each week—when they feel like it—which means they only meditate when certain qualities of mind are present, when they're not distracted by worldly pulls. Thus they only see an easy mind, a mind that wants to sit. They don't see the mind that causes us the most suffering; the mind that's distracted, that wishes it was doing something else. They don't see the mind that's thirsting after satisfaction or that's depressed or lonely, or even the restless, wanting mind that is peering into the icebox or changing channels on the TV, looking for something to watch. They don't see the mind that wants out. Therefore they seldom experience the great power of meditation to cut through negativity and discomfort and open a spacious perspective in which to let go of such bondage.

Sometimes as we try to schedule our day, it may seem difficult to reserve time for meditation. Until we see the value of meditation, it may be difficult to convince ourselves to set aside a period of exploration in the morning and evening. It is very common for such feelings to occur. In Soledad Prison, our group discussed the best schedule for practice. One fellow said that he could sit only for twenty minutes in the morning and not at all in the evening. When I asked him why, he said he just had so much to do with his job, French classes, letter writing, group therapy, and his favorite TV programs that he didn't have time. Several others in the group laughed and pointed out to him that since he was "doing" fifteen years, he had nothing but "time." The poignancy of the moment clearly showed how the mind is constantly seeking satisfaction outside itself and seldom gives itself a chance to become free.

When a daily sitting practice has been established, a general mindfulness becomes noticeable throughout the day. It isn't as moment-to-moment specific as in sitting meditation, because our daily life is so active and filled with old habits and distractions, but slowly the mechanical nature of our reaction to our environment comes into the light of awareness and becomes the basis for continuous practice, whether we're driving a car, cooking a meal, taking care of the children, answering the telephone, or making tea. Whatever we're doing becomes the ground for expanding mindfulness.

At first we discover there is much we're not aware of: like the sensation of our hand on the phone, we don't feel the coldness of the plastic very much; or in lifting the phone, we don't notice the feel of the muscles; or the touching of the earpiece to the ear; or even the intention to speak. As our daily practice expands, awareness opens to encompass more of our activities. As this general mindfulness becomes established, we notice, for instance, that if all of a sudden anger comes up, we are immediately aware of it. It is acknowledged before it is expressed in words or deeds or becomes out of control. We notice ourselves automatically investigating strong interruptions in the flow. We discover that the sooner we are aware of what's going on, the more space we have in which to relate. When we see ourselves about to get lost in a thought or an emotion or desire, we have a moment of choice available, "I've done this ten times before, and I'm always sorry afterward—here it comes again. I think I'll let it go by this time and see what that feels like."

This over-all mindfulness is a general scanning that occurs from having encouraged deeper looking. Painful attitudes and desires have less chance to just appear full-grown in the mind when we can see them coming. It's not what arises in the mind that matters, as much as how soon we are aware—mindful of its presence, how soon the forgetfulness of identification falls away. Even a second can be the difference between being lost in a state of mind and the joy which a moment later says, "There comes that one; how interesting, I'm not pulled by it so much any more." It becomes fascinating because the realization "Wow, I'm free of anger," is often followed by the recognition that we are free from everything at that moment except the pride about how free we are.

As the preciousness of work on ourselves becomes more apparent, we come more purely to the practice. In fact, it is possible for a student who is honestly motivated to gain a great deal from even a less than impeccable teacher because of the power of the purity of the student's participation. Such a student, clear enough to not judge even the seeming impurities of his teacher, cherishing instead the clearest of the teachings which come through, finds wisdom everywhere. Indeed, it is the purity, the selflessness and clarity of intention, which we bring to practice which opens us to the subtlest of teachings. The "secret" of secret teachings is our readiness to hear what is offered; it is the "personal power" of which Don Juan speaks.

A story which illustrates the importance of the attitude we bring to practice involves an old Chinese farmer who after years of wishing to understand more at last hears of a meditation master who is passing through his province. After completing his spring planting, he travels several days on foot seeking this teacher. Coming across the encampment of the teacher and his disciples, he asks for an audience which is granted that afternoon. In great humility he comes before the teacher to request some meditational practice he might work with that will give him some insight, some understanding into the mysteries of life he sees all about him. The master, recognizing the purity of the farmer's motivation, grants his request, and explains to him that the mantra he is about to give him has been empowered by thousands of years of use by monks in monasteries in his homeland. On a scroll, the master writes in Chinese, OM MANI PADME HUM. The farmer is immensely grateful and thanks the master again and again for his help. As the farmer leaves, the master says, "Work with this mantra daily and return to me in a month to tell me how you're doing."

The farmer returns home and immediately unrolls the scroll and begins slowly to read the mantra aloud a few times, to familiarize himself with it. But the Chinese character for "hum" and the character for "cow" are apparently very similar, and the farmer misreads the final word of the mantra as "cow," and begins internalizing his mantra as "Om mani padme *cow*, om mani padme *cow*, om mani padme *cow*."

He works very hard to keep the mantra going, reminding himself again and again to return to practice: when he plows, he plows to the mantra; when he sits, he sits to the mantra; when he draws water, he draws water to the mantra. The more he gives to the mantra, the more his mind is opening, and the deeper his understanding. As the weeks go by, his mind gets clearer and clearer and he feels more and more appreciation for the power of the practice to uncover truth. His life is more spacious, his relationship with his wife and children is better than it has ever been. By the time he is to return to the master, he is happier than he has ever been in his life. Even as he walks the long road back to the master's encampment, he keeps the mantra going: "Om mani padme cow, om mani padme cow."

When he arrives at the master's encampment, he goes directly to the master and says, "I want to thank you so much for giving me this practice. All day long, it's 'om mani padme cow, om mani padme cow' . . ." The master's eyebrows raise two inches and he shouts, "It's what?!! It's not 'om mani padme *cow*,' it's 'om mani padme *hum*.'" He explains to the farmer that the farmer has somehow misunderstood the mantra which the master gave him and that the farmer should honor the way it's been said for thousands of years. He tells the farmer to return home and begin again.

The farmer apologizes profusely and returns home, chagrined and a bit downhearted. Day after day he tries to bring the new mantra to mind, but to little avail. He soon finds his mind filled with confusion and doubt. Returning to the master, dejected and embarrassed, he pleads with the teacher to re-empower his rapidly disintegrating practice. The master smiles to himself, recognizing that the power of the farmer's practice was the farmer's purity of purpose which had been confused in their previous meeting. "For you," the master whispers, "the mantra is 'om mani padme cow, om mani padme cow.'"

There will be times during practice when our purity of intention will be all we have, when no words will be of much help. When it seems as though we are completely lost and without hope, simply noting that state of painful confusion with patience and some considerable tenderness is all that can be done. Just sitting with the moment as it is, when the mind is not clear and we are not able to penetrate some deep distraction, can allow us to open to ourselves in a very generous way. Then we just practice compassion and self-acceptance to continue the purification of mind.

The most a book like this can do is prepare us for an ongoing practice. Reading a book about meditation, like reading a book about swimming, will not assure one of reaching the farthest shore. Words are as shallow as thought —only the direct experience of what is occurring in each moment brings us to a full understanding of the truth. Only by confronting for ourselves the hindrances to our natural wisdom do we gradually begin to awaken.

25

The Flower

As we begin to awaken, we see within us something opening like a flower. We notice that something is displacing
our image of how things are. We discover we're not so
bent on always knowing who we are. It's the experience
that seems to matter most, the being, that we find of value.
It seems as we let go of possessing experience and just let
experience unfold, the flower opens more and more, the
heart opens more and more. And we somehow feel that
everything will be all right, that things are working out just
as they are supposed to. It's painful sometimes, it's ecstatic
sometimes; but somehow it's always perfect. As we penetrate deeper and deeper, it is evident that it is the clarity
of the seeing that nurtures our opening, while the object
observed matters little.

We can't imagine how we ever could have missed seeing
the perfection in the first place, or how we could ever lose it
again. How could we ever again be blind to the simple,
easy, natural, perfect way things are? Experience is simply
experience itself. And if looking into that flower we see a
moment of greed or selfishness or fear, we see it within the
context of that perfection, within that clarity, and it's like

another petal in the flower. We see that it's all natural. Our selfishness doesn't make us feel separate. We see how naturally we're selfish, but there's no self-condemnation. We see it as just how it is. Perfect. No need to be separate because of it. Full of self-forgiveness, full of letting go, full of understanding. It is there, but it's not us. It's just more stuff. There's room in us for all of it.

So at last we are becoming who we always wanted to be, free of much of the guarded self-imagery and neediness that caused so much discomfort in the past. But we see that even this "wonderful me" must be let go of. The being we have become is still separate, though healthier. There's still that subtle "someone" experiencing it all and wanting to keep it opening. There's someone who hasn't altogether merged, hasn't disappeared; still someone looking at the perfection of things. It's then we realize that the flower must die for the fruit to be born.

We recognize that the flower exists on just a subtler level of mind, and that perfection, too, is a concept of how things are and can become a subtle separation which allows for "someone" to watch the perfection of it all. We see that we must let the flower be so it may fall away and leave the fruit.

There is no description possible of the fruit because no matter how we try to describe it, we're still describing the flower. The fruit doesn't exist in mind, in language. Mind gives form to the flower, but clinging to form and mind must be relinquished for the fruit to be revealed, for our original face to come forth.

This fruit, fully ripened in beings like Christ and Buddha, has no seeds, nothing to be reborn, no desires to create karma, no thirst for satisfaction. This fruit does not perish, but remains as an offering for all who come after.

26

A Guided Meditation on Dying

(To be fed slowly to oneself or read aloud to a friend.)

Bring your awareness into the body. Bring your attention to the level of sensation, of feeling, in your body.

Feel the heaviness, the solidness of the head as it rests on the neck. Feel the strength of the neck, its thickness, its substantialness. The flatness and hardness of the shoulders.

Feel the weight of the arms at the shoulders. Feel the denseness of the torso and the body. Feel the thickness of this body-vessel.

Don't grasp at sensation. Just receive what arises in this body we inhabit.

Feel the solidness of it. Feel the pull of gravity as the buttocks rest on the pillow, while the knees touch the floor.

Feel the sensations arising here and there in this form. Multiple tinglings and sensations. They seem to be received by something subtler: a body of awareness which experiences the sensations of the solid body which receives these tinglings and vibrations. A body lighter than this heaviness, than the weightiness of the vessel. A body of light.

Enter this body of awareness, which experiences sound as hearing. Which experiences light as seeing. Which tastes. Which knows life as it's experienced in this heavy form.

Feel . . . sense within this heavy body this lighter body. This light body which receives the sensations produced in the heavier form.

Each breath entering into the heavy body is experienced as sensation by this lighter body. Each breath entering the heavy body sustaining the lighter body, maintaining the balance that allows this body of awareness to remain.

Let the awareness settle very alertly, very carefully, on each in breath, on each out breath. Feel the contact between the heavy body and the light body. Feel the light body cradled in the heavy body, connected and sustained by each breath.

Just awareness and sensation. The experience of life in the body, sustained by the breath.

Experience each breath. Experience this delicate balance moment to moment, as sensation, as awareness itself.

Take each breath as though it were the last.

Experience each inhalation as though it were never to be followed by another. Each breath the last.

Each breath ending without another to follow, severing the connection between the light body and the heavy body. The last breath. The end of a lifetime.

How does mind respond to no more breath, to no more life? What thought of 'no more inhale, exhale'?

Each breath the last. Let go. Don't hold onto it.

Let each breath go. Let yourself die.

Each thought disappearing into space. A lifetime ended. The final moment. Let go. Let yourself die.

Let go of fear. Let go of longing. Open to death. Let go into death. Let yourself die. Die right into this moment. Holding on to nothing. Just die.

Let go of thoughts. Let go of even ideas of dying and living. Just die. Let go completely, and at once.

Go on now. Die gently into the light. Float free.

With an open heart, let go of all the things that hold you back. Let go of your name. Let go of your body. Let go of your mind. Float free. Let yourself die.

Don't be afraid. There's nothing to hold to. Moment after moment, the light body free now. Go on now. Gently go into the light. Free from the dense body, free from this incarnation now.

Float free. Die into the light.

Let go into the pure, open luminosity of your original nature. Just space. Space floating in space. Die into it. Let go. Let altogether go. Go into the light. Just light floating in vast space. Clear mind. Open heart. Let go.

Let go of your knowing. Let go of your not-knowing. All that comes to mind is old. Any thought that arises is just old thought. Float free of all that now. Let yourself die. Just pure awareness. Light itself, experiencing itself within itself. Space within space. Light within light.

Altogether gone. Beyond gone. No inside. No outside. Just is-ness. Just space. Pure awareness. Pure experience. Free of the body. Free of the mind. Die into the open, boundaryless space of your essential purity. Open into it. Let yourself die into the pure light.

Vast space. No boundary. Just let yourself be. Open and endless. Light. Space itself.

Now watch each breath as though it were approaching from far away. As though it were approaching from across vast space.

Each breath the first. Each inhalation the first breath of life. Each moment completely new. Birth.

Consciousness experiencing the body again. Space within space.

Pure awareness reinhabiting pure form. Born again.

Awareness going on moment to moment, just as ever. Experiencing what is. The breath of life once again in the body.

Gently that lightness once again animates the heavy form, takes birth to fulfill its karma, to learn what there is to learn, to be with things as they are.

No death. No birth. No life. Just is-ness. In the body, out of the body. Just is-ness. Just space. Just form. Just formlessness. Experience, a moment at a time.

No life. No death. Just now. Just this.

Entering each moment fully awake. Each moment so precious. All there is.

27

Death of the Body, Death of the Self

When we watch the mind with moment-to-moment awareness, we see one state of mind arise with its own tendencies, its own personality so to speak, its own mood, its associated thoughts; and we see it pass away. And in the following millisecond, we see a whole new mind arise. We see multiple incarnations of mind arising and passing away within our consciousness. We see birth and death. We don't mourn the passing of a state of mind because it's been our experience that another always arises immediately thereafter. Actually, we seldom even see that arising and passing away. We generally experience it as a continuity, a single mind; not seeing that it's continual birth and death, rebirth and redeath. Indeed, what connects one mind moment with the following mind moment is no different from what connects one lifetime with the next. It is the same thing. The unconscious tendencies arise to form one state of mind, then pass away as conditions change, then re-arise as a new mind. Just as when we die that which was the force in the mind, the goals, the aspirations, the desires, continue on to once again re-arise in a new body.

When we observe the rising and passing away of hundreds of incarnations an hour we experience birth and death at a very deep level. Recognizing this moment-to-moment birth and death of the mind allows us to penetrate the illusion of solidity which potentiates the fear of death, the fear of dissolution upon extinction of the physical body. Clearly seeing the ongoing process of one mind leading to another brings deep insight into the perpetuation of awareness after the consciousness principle no longer finds the body a hospitable dwelling place. This deep understanding allows us upon death to know we are dead, to understand how, though the body lies somewhere nearby, consciousness continues. The sooner we recognize we are dead, the better able we will be to navigate within the karmic possibilities provided in the after-death state.

Seeing this moment-to-moment birth and death of the mind allows us to see beyond the death of the transitory body. Seeing the relative nature of life, the greater context in which what we thought to be us actually exists, we begin to experience the death of the self, the diminishment of the power of the following thought to grasp and identify with the previous thought as some solid, separate self. Not identifying hearing as "my hearing," tasting as "my tasting," thinking as "my thinking," but simply recognizing thinking, hearing, tasting, touching as each state of mind arises and passes away of itself, the product of previous conditions, we start to experience the death of the concept of ourselves being someone separate from the flow. As one Zen master put it, "If you haven't come here to die you might as well go home, you're not ready for practice."

As the death of the self begins, we experience the separate self, manifested as personality, to be our distance from each other, our distance from the reality of things as they are, our separation from the being we all share. This great death of separation and fear becomes a very potent force in our lives as we enter a sometimes painful process which reveals that we aren't who we thought we were. And much of what we wished we'd never be, we actually always have been. As the boundaries of who we think we are begin to disintegrate, we allow ourselves to die out of our separateness and experience our oneness with all existence.

The imagined self starts dying when it's no longer potentiated, nurtured, by grasping at experience as its own; when these are simply seen as experiences in the vastness of mind. Mind is seen as the space in which all these things occur. Those are the conditions, the conditionings, of the mind. The mind is a vast spaciousness, by nature inherently pure, which contains everything. All these minds that we experience as ourselves arising and passing away, all these persons that we are, are the content of a much vaster clarity which is not entangled or enmeshed or identified with any of this dance. We get a much broader picture, a much deeper recognition of who we really are, and a deeper understanding of what we die into upon abandonment of the body.

By watching the contents of mind change from one to the other, just seeing change as it flows on, we start to see the process. And when we see the process, we see the frame of reference in which the process is happening. We experience that what we thought to be real before is not so. It's not necessarily unreal, it just isn't real in the same way we had imagined it to be. And our perception of death is markedly altered.

The death of the self may be full of the fear of letting go, of stepping off into the void, thinking that nothing will stop our fall, not recognizing that the void is our true nature. The void is the vastness in which we are occurring, it is the truth itself, and the whole idea of "someone" stepping off is just another bubble passing through. And we don't any longer need to define who we are, because who we become each moment is so much more than what we ever imagined. There's no need to limit who we really are with any definition. We are all of it. And only the contents of this vastness of mind, once identified with as a separate self, limit who we are.

The death of the body is accompanied with much less agony than the death of the self. The death of the self is a tearing away of everything we imagine to be solid, that we had built to deal with the underlying nature of the process which is always change. We've built an imagined self who is constantly filtering the contents of mind, choosing states of mind to be. As that falls away, there's nausea, dizziness. It means the death of everything we learned we were, and all the thoughts and projections that so enamored us in the past, or so created someone to be in the future, are seen as just more natural phenomena of the life flow, arising and passing away within the vastness.

When all we have imagined ourselves to be is seen in its essentially empty, impermanent nature we experience the superficiality of the separate self. When once we see through this dreamlike separateness we recognize that there is in reality no one to die and that it is only the illusion of this separateness which takes birth again and again. Then anything can arise. Loneliness arises, insecurity arises, fear arises, hunger arises, even the longing that drives us from incarnation to incarnation, that creates mind after mind, all of that is seen as just a coming and a going. It is, as the

Diamond Sutra says, "A flash of lightning in a summer cloud, a flickering lamp, a phantom, and a dream."

Then physical death can be honored and respected as a wonderful opportunity, in the passing from one body to another, for awareness to recognize the relativity of everything we imagine to be real, an opportunity for immense breakthrough. Because, as passing out of a body, we see that the body which we thought of as us, the mind which we thought of as us, is quite a bit different, that life itself is a good deal different than we had ever imagined; and a wonderful opportunity for letting go occurs, a great gift which, if used discriminatively, used wisely, can allow much of our desires, much of our fears, much of our sense of separateness, to disintegrate so that nothing separate is left and all that remains is the light entering the light.

It is, I think, as Walt Whitman wrote in *Song of Myself:*

All goes onward and outward, nothing collapses.
And to die is different from what anyone supposed,
and luckier.

28

Spirit in the World

When we see deeply within the silence allowed during sitting, when we see what's always happening but what we're so seldom aware of, we see what a miracle life is. How remarkable it is. Perhaps the more clearly we see what a miracle it is, the more distinctly we encounter the problem of trying to manifest this spirit, these insights, in the world.

For instance, it occurs to me that the cross is a very clear symbol for that predicament. The vertical member of the cross can be seen as the rising of awareness; in some traditions it might even be likened to the spine through which spiritual energy ascends. The horizontal member of the cross is like the arms of man come into the world to manifest his vision, supported by the strength of his spiritual awareness. It is through these arms that the inner wisdom is realized in the outer world, that the work is shared in service and care.

It is not coincidence that Christ was crucified on the convergence of the inner world of the rising spirit and the outer world of need all about us. His heart radiates compassion at the very center of the juncture of these two realities. For many of us this is a very powerful mirror for our own predicament, because there's a great deal of confusion, of wondering, about how to properly actualize this growing understanding, this gradual awakening for the benefit of others while still meeting worldly responsibilities.

"What is right livelihood?" is the question most often asked by people as they start to awaken. "Where do I find a job that is useful to others, that causes no injury, that allows a fair give and take? Knowing that, for me, it's not becoming the boss or one-upping the neighbors that counts, how do I make sufficient money to live and support those I love while still being helpful to others?" As this question gains intensity, the symbol of the cross becomes all the more recognizable, for it can be seen that the image of Christ contains both the personification of this dilemma and the path leading to its resolution: Christ's method of awakening is the method of the heart. It is by listening with the heart that we hear what is appropriate in the moment.

In the Noble Eightfold Path, the Buddha mapped out three aspects of working clearly in the world: right speech, right action, and right livelihood. Those are three means of manifesting insight, of manifesting awakening in the world. How do we do so? Well, we make our action mindful, we try to stay aware of what we're doing. We stay in our body. We watch our mind. We know our action and we know our thought. We pay attention to our speech. We keep our speech from gossip. We keep speech from being slanderous. We keep it truthful. We keep our actions from hurting others. We don't steal or kill. For our livelihood, we take jobs that aren't harmful to ourselves or to others. Traditionally, the Buddha recommended that we not take jobs as trappers, hunters, or fishers, or work in a place that makes weapons or encourages war.

But we needn't go to scripture to know what the heart signals. If we pay attention, it becomes all too clear that there is enough suffering in the world without adding to it. We don't want to work in a slaughterhouse, we don't want to be an executioner; we want to alleviate distress, not cause it. We see that right livelihood begins in the heart; that the resolution of the question about work in the world is *how* to work more on ourselves, how to make every action a further opportunity for practice. When we're investigating what right livelihood is, we're no longer meditating only when we're sitting. The meditation encompasses the whole day.

Part of our growing wakefulness is a growing kindness, an openheartedness, a gentleness. How can I maintain grace-fulness and survive in a society that doesn't particularly value such qualities? Some become nurses or social workers or work in the "helping professions," and are of use to many. But no matter what job we take—even the most seemingly pure job—every day there are going to be those questions, "How much more purely could I be manifesting my energies? How much more truthful, how much less grasping could I be today?"

The question of right livelihood is not just a question of right income; it's a question of right living. That word "livelihood" goes much deeper than how we get our pay check. It's how we manifest the spirit in all ways. It's clear action.

Real morality comes from the heart, from sensing what's appropriate in the moment. The question of right action is not a cut-and-dried dictum that applies to all situations in every instance. Therefore, in most discussions of right action there usually occurs some question about killing. Is no killing appropriate? How about weeding the lawn? Or, what if one discovers something like body lice? What about killing for food? What about mercy killing? Does all killing block the light?

Certainly, in any intentional act of killing, if we watch the mind closely, it's quite clear that at the moment of killing an aggressive energy is present, a separation exists between us and what we're killing. But we know what's right for us because we can feel it in our heart. If we're staying in our heart, if we're paying attention to how we really feel, we can feel from thought to thought what's wholesome or unwholesome, what's useful and outgoing and what's obstructive.

An example of trying to work in the world while staying in the heart though confronted with a difficult problem is of a friend who felt she had to have an abortion. She already had a child and was having a very hard time relating to her. Many people around her agreed that if she brought another child into the world it would have perhaps pushed her over the edge. Her psychiatrist and others quite readily supported her negative expectations, which decided it for her. She could not see or hear any alternative. She told me, "I have to have an abortion: the doctor says I should have it, so does the psychiatrist, even the father said so, everybody agrees I mustn't have this child." So, we talked about the possibility of her having an abortion with the same affirming consciousness one would bring to a birth, to really wish that being well in its passage through; how she could have the abortion with the greatest love possible, with kindness for herself, recognizing how easy

it might be to get waylaid by guilt. Offering herself understanding and kindness and a loving acceptance, and using
the moment as work on herself instead of just causing herself more suffering and self-hatred, separation and grief,
she later told me it was one of the most powerful experiences of her life, one of the most beautiful experiences
she had ever had. It was, for her, a healing. She had done
the best she could under the circumstances. She had sent
love in a situation in which she might have manifested
great anger and self-hatred. She came into the light as perfectly as possible.

If we listen to our hearts and watch our actions, we learn
from ourselves. We learn where we have work to do. We
don't have to superimpose any "do's" and "don'ts." We discover for ourselves that the truth has no single form, that
truth is only in the moment and can always be discovered
right there. There's no reality to create. There's only a reality to tune in to.

As we tune in more and more to our heart, to ourselves,
we discover that there's also a silent transmission of heart
between people. The heart recognizes that words are often
an excuse for people to communicate while the real communication is taking place. Indeed, words sometimes even
block the heart by keeping the reception only in the mind,
instead of allowing it to be sensed from that place where
we can experience another person within ourselves. When
we experience that deep connection of intuitive mind to
intuitive mind, the separation between beings melts away
and communication has less to do with words.

There can be a transmission between two beings that is so
deep that words, any words, would just disturb that openheartedness. This subtle transmission of the heart can be

experienced when we're with someone we care for very much. I have experienced it with my children and loved ones, as well as with dying patients I have been working with.

Instead of speaking aloud, we find we can send thoughts silently through the heart. At first, being completely honest, we might find ourselves saying, "I don't even know how to do this, but here I am. What I'm trying to do is send love, send care to you through my heart. I'm not trying to change you, I'm just loving you as best I can." Later, as this subtle communication develops, it will be like doing the loving-kindness meditation. We may well work with thoughts such as, "Just as I wish to be free of suffering and to be openhearted, so may you come to your wholeness, your joy." We can sometimes even do this with animals and notice a response. Sometimes that sharing will be very clearly received by a person and a mood change will occur, the whole vibration in the room will change. Often, things we can never say because of awkwardness, inhibition, and doubt can be said through the heart. It's not the words that are communicated, it's the intentions; it's the state of mind that is communicated, it's the attitude of caring.

Through the heart, we can transmit our growing awareness and our respect for others' growth; we can share the spirit with another. We can communicate our caring without getting lost in the magic of it; with a pure intention that opens out to others, that brings the heart into the world: the merging of the inner and outer realities, the essence of compassion and right action.

As we develop this communication, we find that not only are we more able to speak through the heart, but that we are also more able to hear it, to receive more through the heart. We notice that we can more clearly sense the appropriate response to the conditions of the moment, that right livelihood is a clearer, less problematic path and the joy of it widens access to the wisdom mind. Clearly, the heart opens the mind just as the mind opens the heart: right livelihood.

29

Practice at Work

In the course of teaching meditation with Elisabeth Kübler-Ross, she asked me to visit some of her dying patients. Very soon it became clear that working with the dying was a means of working on myself. In the flow of this work I met an extraordinary Dominican nun, Sister Patrice Burns, with whom I worked for a few months in the cancer ward of a San Francisco hospital. When I first came to the hospital, it was obvious to me how my practice was being put to the test. As one Zen teacher put it, "Your practice is fit for calm, but is it fit for disturbance?" And another teacher asked, "Can you keep your heart open in Hell?"

I found that a hospital is probably the most difficult environment in which to afford a really good death. Hospitals are meant to preserve life; death is an enemy there. Death is not treated with much respect, with much compassion. There's a lot of fear surrounding death. Death is a failure in a hospital.

Most terminally ill patients say they wish not to be alone when they are approaching death. They want access to people, not to feel cut off. However, in many hospitals because of a lack of understanding of how to work with the dying and how to accept their own dying, nurses and doctors and technicians are often not available in any meaningful way to a dying patient. Studies have shown that, not willfully, but because of our subtle psychological tendencies, the call-light of a terminal patient takes longer to be answered by the nursing staff than that of a patient whom the nurses sense they can "do something to help." Therefore, at the time of our greatest hope for contact with life, we have the least opportunity. Not such a good place to die.

It became clear to me that the problem in hospitals is the same as the problem in ourselves: ignorance. A lack of understanding of the ongoing process. It's fear and resistance personified, concretized in attitudes and in separation from some part of ourselves we don't comprehend: our dying.

I saw that a good nurse on a ward became a blessing to her patients, and made a great deal of difference. Actually "good nurse" is not the right term. What I mean is a nurse who is in touch with herself enough to allow herself to care. In many nursing schools, and in much medical training, it's very common to hear, "Don't get involved with your patients." However, it is that quality of caring, of involvement, that is the essence of healing. Essentially what is happening in hospitals and in the medical profession in general is that healing is taken out of the human realm, out of the realm of the transmission of energy, and put into the chemical-electrical realm of medicines and devices.

I experienced how difficult it is to care with as much ignorance as we usually carry with us most of the time.

How easily we identify with our conditioning about dying and how painful it is when we lose our perspective about suffering. I know very few people who work with the dying who aren't deeply affected and often fatigued by it. It is very demanding work. Only when we can see life and death as not so separate, as part of an ongoing process of maturation, of coming home, of returning to God, of returning to the source—whatever terms we try to define this process with—can we stay mindful of the context in which the pain and dying are occurring. Then, when working with someone who's in pain, we honor their difficulty, we see how difficult it is for them, but we don't reinforce their resistance to that pain by saying how awful pain is and therefore intensify their affliction. Nor do we say, "Oh the pain is just due karmic process," because that is not compassion. We're just talking off the top of our head, we're not working on ourselves by encouraging that state of mind which maintains separation. It *is* their karma, but that understanding has to come from a deep experience of the moment, from the heart, not from the head. We have to feel it as our karma, not just as their karma. We have to discover karma in ourselves, not as a concept, but as an ongoing experience, as an unfolding. Our unfolding, their unfolding: all part of the same process. The content of our life and their life might be different, just as the content of our mind and another person's mind is different, but the process is precisely the same. The natural laws governing cause and effect and the laws governing how the mind and body relate are precisely the same. And it's that sameness that is the way into understanding, the way not to get caught in content, our content or their content. In fact, it is on the level of that sameness where contact can be made.

That sameness exists when I walk into the room of a person who is in great pain, and I feel it in my gut, but the feeling is surrounded by a spaciousness which is just with it as it is, which is willing to allow it to follow its natural course. It can be psychological pain like anger or fear or great doubt, or it can be cancer eating their nervous system. In the room there is extreme discomfort, extreme dissatisfaction with the present. And I sit with them, and let myself go into that feeling. But I go into it taking with me the understanding of the process of the context in which we all exist. And entering that experience as much as I might, I pass through it, allowing them to pass through it when they can. These words certainly don't convey the experience. But as I'm sitting with somebody, I can let go into them, I seem almost to become them. I'm not someone separate from them; the distance between me and the person I'm with is not an obstacle to my ability to be available to them. Which means giving up some image of myself as some great white knight, as Captain Karma, come to heal the sick and dying, with some subtle denial in my head that I am sick and dying, that I am riddled with clinging and ignorance. I am wise; they are not. I am healthy; they are ill. This is delusion.

Buddha said that fortune changes like the swish of a horse's tail. Two beings are in that room and they're there karmically. One is down and heading out of this life, the other one's there because there's nowhere else he can be of more use to himself or someone else. We both have work to do on ourselves. If we're in that room under any other pretext, we are not getting the most out of the situation. It's the same whatever we're doing; it's just more evident when we're with ourself dying.

A person's in the room with me who is very close to dying, and afraid. I can feel the fear of death in myself. In working through my fear, I give them an opportunity, silent though it may be, to work through theirs. If I come into a room, saying, "Oh, there's nothing to be afraid of: we go through death and then into another rebirth," that's not very useful. That's a way of not dealing with the power of the moment—the suffering in that room in the fellow on the bed, and the suffering in the mind of the fellow next to the bed.

It's the ability to suffer, the ability to experience my own unsatisfactory mind, my own unfortunate resultant karma—that is the ability to purify and get done. Working with the dying is like facing a finely polished, very fierce mirror of my own reality. Because I see my fears, and how much I dislike pain. The conditioned dislike of pain, of uncomfortable mental and physical states, is very great— it's going to be something we're working with much of the time. The judging mind is leaning over my shoulder, telling me how uncooked I am, how much work I have to do on myself. If I stay open to it, sometimes it gets quite painful but it's obviously the work that is to be done, so I stay with it, and sometimes find myself very open-minded, soft, compassionate, and very present.

The attachment which wants someone to die some other way than the way they are dying is of no use to them; that's my problem. I learned not to make someone else die my death for me. Not bringing my problems into the room became the process for further purification. Sometimes if

I'm with a person and I'm stuck, I just have to say, "I'm stuck now," but that's more honesty than that person may experience all day. There's a lot of pretense in hospital rooms. The person lying in bed is often pretending, the people visiting are pretending. My work in that room is simply one of being. No pretense. And to be, I must be present. I have to be able to accept all of myself. And part of me is suffering and lying in that bed. In truth there are two deaths occurring right then.

Honesty doesn't mean forcing my truth on someone. It means being present, being real. I could feel that the more open I was, the more accepting of the human condition, of the suffering that comes with our involuntary grasping, from our immense forgetfulness, the more space I was able to allow for our growth. And the more compassion I had for even my own projections and fears. I could see that compassion is not interference. It is not forcing someone into my karma. Compassion comes from feeling another's suffering and transcending it in myself, leaving them the open space into which to grow, or even die, as they see fit, as they can, as they're karmically able.

I found that compassion meant not saying, "Oh, how nice you look today," when they were getting grayer and thinner, but rather letting them be sick when they *were* sick. Letting them accept themselves. Not to reinforce their aversion for their sickness because their sickness is what they have to work with. It's their method.

I saw how much we underrate the capacity of the human heart, how we think we can only be of service through knowing something. But the intuitive understanding of the wisdom mind can allow us to be available to another without getting lost in a lot of "doing." We're just there, because we're open to be there. Which means someone is deathly ill and we accept their sickness and take that, too, into our heart. When the pain in the room is so great it pries open the heart, by not holding onto things being any way other than they actually are we seem almost to disappear at that point where the heart and mind coincide—we experience ourselves within the open heart of understanding. We feel the other person as ourselves, and speak to them as though speaking to ourselves. Then even the technique of talking through the heart mentioned elsewhere becomes a technique of talking to ourself.

At those moments when I was no longer being "the giver," or even giving, but was just there as two aspects of myself, one dying and one watching, I was reunited with my completeness, and all fatigue vanished. I was fed from the same source, from the no-mind spaciousness of something greater than my limited "me" which was feeding another.

When we're giving from the source and we come out of the room, we don't even know who we are. There is so much spaciousness of mind, we just don't know. The person dies, and we don't even know if we helped. We did what we could and learned from it, but we don't even know what we learned. All we know is that there was a process going on, a process of moving toward our vastness, toward our potential, toward being who we hardly even imagined we are.

30

The Circle

We sit in a circle. This has great significance for in a circle, all points are equal.

The circle is the form of nature. In nature, all things move in cycles. There are the seasons, day and night, life and death. Light moves into darkness, returning to light.

The American Indian spoke of the Great Hoop, in which all people were protected. When the hoop was broken, people no longer lived within the cyclical nature of who they were, and they lost their "knowingness," their contact with the flow. The Indian nations were scattered and nearly destroyed.

Energy seems to move in circles: the orbiting of the planets, the cycling of electrons around the nucleus of the atom. When we come into the circle, we come into the flow. But we push against that circle, when we try to think "circle," or think "flow," we make it linear with a beginning and an end, we distort it.

Each moment is a perfect circle. When we penetrate into the totality of the moment, we see that no point on that circle has any better vantage for seeing the rest of the circle than any other point. We see that each moment is the perfect outcome of all that has come before, the perfect predecessor of all that will follow.

Our sitting becomes like entering a perfect circle in which there is room for everything. We never become lost because there's nowhere to go. We are constantly arriving home in the present moment.

Surrender is perfect participation in the circle. Letting go allows us to flow, to become the whole circle. To hold to any point on the circle is to lose our original nature because there is no place we begin and nowhere we end.

Suggested Reading

Babbitt, Irving. *The Dhammapada*. New York: New Directions.

Blofeld, John. *The Zen Teachings of Huang Po*. New York: Grove Press.

Castaneda, Carlos. *Journey to Ixtlan*. New York: Simon & Schuster.

Chogyam Trungpa. *Meditation in Action*. Berkeley, California: Shambhala.

——. *Cutting Through Spiritual Materialism*. Berkeley, California: Shambhala.

——. *The Myth of Freedom*. Berkeley, California: Shambhala.

——, with F. Fremantle. *The Tibetan Book of the Dead*. Berkeley: Shambhala.

The Diamond Sutra and the Sutra of Hui Neng. Berkeley, California: Shambhala.

Goldstein, Joseph. *The Experience of Insight*. Santa Cruz, California: Unity Press.

Goleman, Daniel. *Varieties of the Meditative Experience*. New York: E. P. Dutton.

Kornfield, Jack. *Living Buddhist Masters.* Santa Cruz, California: Unity Press.

Krishnamurti, J. *Freedom from the Known.* New York: Harper & Row.

——. *Commentaries on Living.* Third Series. London: V. Gollancz.

Kübler-Ross, Elisabeth. *Death: The Final Stage of Growth.* New York: Prentice-Hall.

Lao Tzu. *Tao Te Ching.* D. C. Lau (trans.) Baltimore, Maryland: Penguin. Blackney (trans.) New York: Mentor.

Lerner, Eric. *A Journey of Insight Meditation.* New York: Schocken.

Merton, Thomas. *The Way of Chuang Tzu.* New York: New Directions.

Nyanaponika Thera. *The Heart of Buddhist Meditation.* New York: Samuel Weiser.

Osborne, Arthur (ed.). *The Teachings of Ramana Maharshi.* New York: Samuel Weiser.

Ram Dass. *Be Here Now.* New York: Crown.

——. *The Only Dance There Is.* New York: Doubleday/Anchor Books.

——. *The Journey of Awakening.* New York: Bantam Books.

——, with Stephen Levine. *Grist for the Mill.* Santa Cruz, California: Unity Press.

Reps, Paul. *Zen Flesh, Zen Bones.* New York: Doubleday/Anchor Books.

Seung Sahn. *Dropping Ashes on the Buddha.* New York: Grove Press.

Sujata, A. *Beginning to See.* Santa Cruz, California: Unity Press.

Suzuki, Shunryu. *Zen Mind, Beginner's Mind*. New York: Weatherhill.

Tartang Tulku. *Calm and Clear*. Emeryville, California: Dharma Press.

———. *Gesture of Balance*. Emeryville, California: Dharma Press.

Wei Wu Wei. *Posthumous Pieces*. Hong Kong: Hong Kong University Press.

Index

In the mid-1970s, while working with Ram Dass (*Grist for the Mill*, 1976) and teaching meditation in the California prison system, STEPHEN LEVINE met Elisabeth Kübler-Ross. For the next few years he led workshops with her and learned from the terminally ill the need for deeper levels of healing and the profound joy of service (*A Gradual Awakening*, 1979). In 1980 he began teaching workshops with his wife, Ondrea, as they continued to serve the terminally ill and those deeply affected by loss as Co-Directors of the Hanuman Foundation Dying Project (*Who Dies?*, 1982). For three years, Ondrea and Stephen maintained a free-consultation telephone line for those confronting serious illness or the possible death of a loved one (*Meetings at the Edge*, 1984). As the Levines continued to gain insight from those who overcame illness and surpassed death, their explorations deepened while further meditative techniques were developed to "let the healing in." Their guided meditations for the healing of illness, grief holdings, heavy emotional states, and sexual abuse and subtler forms of life/death preparation brought them international recognition (*Healing into Life and Death*, 1987), having aided thousands of people worldwide. Presently Stephen and Ondrea Levine are living in the high mountains of the Southwest, "attempting to practice what we preach" in the silence of the deep woods. They are seeking the "healing we took birth for," working on a new book, feeding the animals and the trees, and "examining the weatherbeaten outcroppings and the sun-dappled forests of the mind, sipping at the clear wellsprings of the heart."